THE ACCOUNTABILITY CIRCLE

THE ACCOUNTABILITY CIRCLE

DISCOVERING YOUR TRUE PURPOSE,
POTENTIAL, AND IMPACT...WITH
ACCOUNTABILITY PARTNERSHIPS

SAM SILVERSTEIN

To my life's accountability partner, my wife, Renee.

ACKNOWLEDGMENTS

JUST AS WE GROW to be our very best with the help of other people, our accountability partners, projects like this only happen with the help of other people.

The accountability partners in my life have made a huge impact on me. In particular, I would like to thank Mike Domitrz. Not only did Mike take the time to contribute his story to this book, but he gets on the phone with me every day to share, discuss, help, serve, care, guide, listen, and love. You are a blessing in my life.

David Wildasin and the entire team at Sound Wisdom made this book a reality. You get behind my projects, make them look great, and make it possible to deliver important messages to the world. Thank you for your commitment to my writing.

My personal editor, Cara Wordsmith, Ltd., works tirelessly to help make my books the very best they can be. It is a joy to work closely on projects like this.

And to you the reader—thank you for continuing to seek out my books, to read them, and for all the stories you send me about how you are using what I share. I so appreciate you.

Published and distributed by:
SOUND WISDOM
P.O. Box 310
Shippensburg, PA 17257-0310
717-530-2122

info@soundwisdom.com

www.soundwisdom.com

Cover/jacket design by Geoff Silverstein

ISBN 13 TP: 978-1-64095-174-7

ISBN 13 eBook: 978-1-64095-175-4

For Worldwide Distribution, Printed in the U.S.A.

1 2 3 4 5 6 7 8 / 24 23 22 21 20

Contents

PART I

WHY AN ACCOUNTABILITY CIRCLE?

CHAPTER 1

A **SPECIAL** PLACE

 WE DON'T KNOW WHAT OUR OWN POTENTIAL IS

If we allow ourselves the opportunity to let others around us illuminate our potential, we can become who we were meant to be. What once seemed like miracles can be within our reach.

WE ALL WANT TO GET the most out of our potential. We all want to get the most we possibly can out of life. We all want to become the person we were meant to be and make the impact and contribution we are supposed to make. And we all want to leave a legacy that inspires other people to be their best self also.

For most of us, the problem is not that we do not try to be our best. The real problem is that we are unable to fully see and understand what our very best can be. We think that we have to create our own solutions, that we cannot ask for help. No one can be their best in a vacuum. People are naturally inspired and motivated to be their very best when they are around other people doing the same.

We can become our best possible self only when we are helping others to be their best possible self. Unless we are helping other people, we are not making the most of our own potential.

As the great Jewish sage and scholar Rabbi Hillel put it over two millennia ago, "If I am not for myself, who will be for me? If I am only for myself, what am I? And if not now, when?" These questions are the Accountability Circle in essence.

We have been taught that accountability is something that we can use against other people or that can be used against us to ensure the completion of one or more specific tasks, e.g., "I am holding you accountable for hitting your sales quota." But everything we have been taught about accountability is wrong. Accountability is not a way of doing. Accountability is a way of thinking. Specifically, it is how we think about our relationships with people.

ACCOUNTABILITY IS NOT ABOUT CONTROLLING OTHERS

The phrase "I am holding you accountable" reflects a deeply flawed understanding of accountability.

Accountability is about our commitments to people, our approach to relationships, and our willingness to be interdependent.

"IF I AM ONLY FOR MYSELF, WHAT AM I?"

 We are responsible for things. We are accountable to people. In order to achieve our own potential, we must help other people be their very best... and we must accept their help in becoming our very best. Accountability is the fulfillment of this principle and the practical application of these wise words:

"If I am not for myself, who will be for me? If I am only for myself, what am I? And if not now, when?"

—Rabbi Hillel

Action always follows belief. When you believe that accountability is not about "holding someone accountable," but rather about helping someone be accountable by honoring your own commitments first, then you start to see people differently and you start to act differently. And you get a different result.

When you believe that accountability is not about limiting yourself or others but rather about creating committed relationships based on integrity, then you will commit differently and you will bring people into your life differently. Ultimately, you will build accountable relationships and open yourself up to opportunities for growth that before were unseen and unrealized.

The way to bring committed, accountable relationships into your life is through an Accountability Circle. This book shows you how to do that.

An Accountability Circle allows you to discover how your best self is seen through the eyes of people who truly care about you...

before you even realize who your best self is! This discovery results, not just in deeper and more meaningful relationships within the Circle of Allies you will be creating, but in the capacity to contribute more, create more, and do more in all of your relationships *outside* the Circle—so that you can achieve critical life goals and make deeper contributions in your home life, in your workplace, and in the larger world. By acknowledging your interdependence with others, you grow faster, become more than you expected, and achieve greater and more meaningful goals than you imagined yourself capable of. That is the power of an Accountability Circle.

A SPECIAL PLACE

When we talk about being part of an Accountability Circle, we are talking about creating a special place that helps everyone in the Circle be the best they can possibly be, in all aspects of life.

This is a place defined by the presence and engagement of a few people who have self-selected to support each other in pursuing that goal. These people are called Accountability Partners.

Understand: The Accountability Circle is not just about best practices, not just about tactics, not just about what we are doing to move forward in our careers or grow our businesses. All of that may enter into the conversation. But in an Accountability Circle there is something much deeper going on. Here, we ask questions like:

 Who are we really as people?

👉 Who could we be?

👉 How can I impact this world?

👉 What is the legacy I am leaving and/or could leave?

👉 Why do I choose to take the actions I take?

👉 How can I help you become the best person you can possibly be?

👉 And how can you help me become the best person I can possibly be?

PURPOSE, MISSION, VALUES

In order for an Accountability Circle to function, it has to be rooted in an intimate, caring, mutually supportive relationship with all of your Accountability Partners. The way you build and sustain such relationships is by having increasingly honest conversations, held in confidence, about three things that are unique to each of us as individuals—our Purpose, our Mission, and our Values.

If you are like most of the people with whom I work, you may have only a vague sense of how these three terms differ from each other or how they apply to your life. An Accountability Circle gives you total clarity about each one. This book leads you to that clarity.

CLARITY

In order to be part of an Accountability Circle, you must have total clarity about what your Purpose is, what your Mission in life is, and what your Values are. This book leads you to that clarity.

When you accept someone into your Accountability Circle, what you are really doing is saying, "I agree to talk about what matters most in my life; I agree to be transparent with you about my Purpose, my Mission, and my Values, as well as the actions I am taking in support of them. I expect you to do the same, and I expect you to be equally transparent with me about your Purpose, your Mission, your Values, and what you are doing to support them. And we agree to celebrate our successes and support each other with the truth whenever we see a problem."

With that agreement in place, you get to know people in your Accountability Circle more deeply than you get to know most other people. You build a bond that becomes stronger over time. The people in your Circle know you are there for them, and vice versa. You all agree to share everything of consequence that is going on. You are there for the best of times, and you all agree to help each other deal with the various obstacles that arise.

To put it simply: In an Accountability Circle, you are all deeply committed to making sure everyone in the Circle knows, and stays in alignment with, their Purpose, their Mission, and their Values.

Each one of you is deeply committed to keeping the Accountability Circle a safe place. The Circle has to be safe in two ways. First, it has to be safe for me to show up and say, "I have a problem. Something is not right. I am having trouble in such-and-such an area. I am not sure what to do. I need your feedback." That is the first kind of safety.

It also has to be safe for someone in the Circle to say, "Hey, Sam, I have to say something. From where I sit, what you are talking about doing in such-and-such an area does not match up with what you say your Purpose is. Can we talk about that?" Being a member of an Accountability Circle carries with it, not just the right, but the *duty*, to initiate some sort of intervention when we see someone going in a direction that we feel does not support them.

We are not necessarily talking about crisis situations (although we could be) but about *anything* that is going on in your life that could be taking you off course. If I am a part of your Accountability Circle and I think I see you going off course, I have to speak up, and I have to feel safe as I speak up.

WHAT MAKES ACCOUNTABILITY CIRCLES WORK?

You cannot be part of a functioning Accountability Circle without sharing, at a very deep level, what is most important to you and why—and then listening to what others have to say about how you are taking action on what you say is important to you. By the same token, you cannot be part of an Accountability Circle without learning what is deeply important to the other people in the Circle, why that is important to them, and how they are going to take action. This requires shared trust at a deep level. Trust is what makes Accountability Circles work.

What your Purpose in life is, what Mission supports that Purpose, what Values guide you as you strive to fulfill that Mission, whether your decisions and life choices support the kind of person you say you want to be—these are highly personal things. When we enter into an Accountability Circle, we agree to share *all* of those things, and we agree to listen when someone in the Circle sees us going off course, in matters big or small.

Notice that we do not make these kinds of agreements with everyone we meet. We make and keep such agreements only with people we know well, people who will respect and protect what we tell them in confidence, people who expect the same respect and protection from us. This is what makes Accountability Partners special people: they will always tell us the truth, no matter what, and they will always tell us that truth sensitively, with discretion, and without delay or equivocation.

This is true intimacy. Notice that (for instance) a mastermind group or a business networking group is simply not designed to sustain this level of intimacy. In most cases, these groups are essentially tactical. They are about sharing best practices and connections, and that is good. An Accountability Circle, by contrast, is designed to make it safe for the members to be able to speak up when they notice someone in the Circle taking any action that does not support their growth and development as individuals.

That kind of relationship is possible only when you get to know someone over time on a very deep level. An Accountability Circle is the ultimate trust relationship.

TRUST

An Accountability Circle is the ultimate trust relationship.

So what does that level of trust produce? First and foremost, it produces an assumption of goodwill.

In an Accountability Circle, I know that if you choose to tell me something about how you think I may have gone off track, you are telling me that only because you care for me as a person. You say what you say because you care about whether I become the best possible version of myself, *period*. You have no ulterior motive. That means I can listen and hear you differently than I would if I thought you were sharing something in order to gain some sort of social, career, or financial advantage. I can react differently to the feedback you share with me, I can make better decisions, and I can move forward faster—all because you feel safe sharing something that you think will benefit me, and I feel safe receiving what you have to say.

Second, that level of trust and intimacy produces *directness*. You have made a commitment to share what I need to hear in a way that I can easily understand and quickly act on it. This is not a judgment call. You do not brood about it or debate whether you should say something. You *must* share your concerns with me when they arise because you have made a commitment to me that you are going to do that. And I *must* listen to you because I have made a commitment to listen. As a result, I, in turn, feel safe bringing up anything that I think is important for *you* to hear right away. We do not delay. We do not make excuses. We remember Rabbi Hillel's question: "If not now, when?" And we both grow as people.

That kind of growth occurs only where there is a deeply trusting relationship, a relationship based on specific commitments that are upheld over time. This is the kind of relationship you build, and sustain, in an Accountability Circle.

If you want to learn how to take part in an Accountability Circle... keep reading.

ACCOUNTABILITY TAKEAWAYS: CHAPTER 1

We are responsible for things. We are accountable to people.

Accountability is about our commitments to people, our approach to relationships, and our willingness to be interdependent. In order to achieve our own potential, we must help other people be their very best...and we must accept their help in becoming our very best. Accountability is the fulfillment of this principle and the practical application of these wise words:

"If I am not for myself, who will be for me? If I am only for myself, what am I? And if not now, when?"

An Accountability Circle is a group of trusted, carefully chosen people who commit to helping us become the person we are meant to be, even if that means saying something we do not particularly want to hear or pointing out something we do not particularly want to see. We agree to do the same for them.

This is a small group of Allies who agree to connect with each other on a regular basis to discuss and uphold specific commitments.

Within this Circle, everyone commits to identifying and discussing in detail how well they are aligning with their Purpose, their Mission, and their Values.

This is the most powerful support group there is.

If you want to learn how to take part in an Accountability Circle...keep reading.

CHAPTER 2

TWO BIG QUESTIONS
ABOUT
ACCOUNTABILITY CIRCLES

TWO QUESTIONS I hear a lot about Accountability Circles are:

- I have close friends I feel I can share anything with. Isn't that the same thing?

- What is the difference between what you are talking about and a mastermind group?

Let's tackle the first question first.

CLOSE FRIENDS

Having a very close friend is *not* the same thing as being in an Accountability Circle. The reason for this is very simple. Even someone with whom we are very close may feel hesitant about saying something they know we do not want to hear. That is because the specific commitments that support accountability have not been agreed upon in clear, unambiguous terms. Without these commitments, there is wiggle room, and where there is wiggle room, there is a lack of accountability. There is no wiggle room in an Accountability Circle.

NO WIGGLE ROOM

Where there is wiggle room, there is a lack of accountability. Accountability Circles are all about eliminating wiggle room. We either make a commitment or we do not. We are either fulfilling that commitment or we are not.

If a close friend knows that you are unwilling to discuss the impact of a decision and there are no clear agreements to appeal to in support of raising that uncomfortable topic, whatever it might be, the friend will tend to shy away from that topic. It takes an explicit agreement that makes raising uncomfortable topics not only okay, but mandatory, for the relationship to be part of an Accountability Circle. Determining what those agreements look like and how best to uphold them is what this book is all about.

For instance, suppose Paul is your best friend, and you feel comfortable sharing anything with him. Suppose Paul is married, with two kids. Suppose Paul tells you that his guiding Values are Honesty, Integrity, and Transparency in all his relationships. And suppose you happen to find out that Paul has been having an affair and concealing that affair from his wife. Suppose, too, that Paul has responded angrily and emotionally whenever questions about his personal life have come up in your discussions.

What safety do you have within that relationship to point out that Paul is out of alignment with his stated Values? None. Even though you and Paul are close, even though you spend a lot of time together, even though you feel comfortable sharing things with him, there are no explicit commitments that support you beginning this important, sensitive, confidential dialogue. You risk damaging or destroying the friendship if you raise the issue. Paul has created wiggle room.

This is not to say that a close friend cannot *become* a part of your Accountability Circle—many times they do. But it is important to understand that the kind of close, mutually supportive relationship we are talking about does not happen without explicit agreements, made out loud, to address all the relevant issues. You can have a very close friendship, but if you ever find yourself avoiding saying something you know the person needs to hear and act on, you can be sure it is not yet a truly accountable relationship.

MASTERMIND GROUPS

Let's look next at the mastermind group. This is a gathering of like-minded professionals who meet regularly to share insights, advice, and best practices. Here again, we cannot assume the presence of explicit agreements about our unique personal Values, our shared commitments, and our integrities for communicating effectively within the group. The following true story may help illuminate the vast difference between a mastermind group and an Accountability Circle.

A dear friend of mine named Mike Domitrz, someone I have known for many years and who is now one of my Accountability Partners, happened to be in the same mastermind group I was in. Each of us was (and is) a professional speaker. We had been in this group for several years, and we each felt we had gotten something positive out of it.

While the group started its journey by focusing on both personal and professional development, over time the mastermind group became more focused on providing very specific tactical how-to discussions for growing each other's businesses. The group got very good at this. Some of the members also became very good at networking and working together on business projects. The focus of the group, it became clear, was on driving revenue increases for the members' businesses. That is a perfectly valid goal, of course, but the intense focus on it seemed to have changed the tone of the discussions. On one of our calls, Mike shared with the group his strong feeling that he was looking for more than techniques, business connections, and strategies. He was seeking to dive deep into both personal and professional development.

I felt the same way.

Shortly after that meeting, Mike called me up and said, "I am just not getting out of these meetings what I want. Are you?" I had to agree that I was not either.

We took some time and thought back on the group's history, and we concluded that while there had been no shortage of discussions about how to grow one's business in the previous incarnations of this group, what had really made a difference for us was the group's past willingness to focus on personal development goals, goals that extended beyond this month's or this quarter's sales and revenue projections. And now sales and revenue were all we seemed to be talking about.

Mike and I talked privately for a while about what was going on, and we realized that in the group as it was currently constituted, there was not the level of deep trust and intimacy that made personal disclosure comfortable. As a result, there was not much room in that mastermind group for discussions about our personal Values, our long-term commitments, and our major life goals. It is hard to get highly personal and share vulnerabilities when others in the room are not doing the same, or if you feel that what you share is being judged.

The focus was on solving specific, narrowly defined business problems. And we realized that was the way it was in most mastermind groups, for the simple reason that intimate discussions were not what most people joining such groups wanted out of the sessions. They wanted access to the insights and expertise of others so that they could solve the most pressing short-term problems on their to-do list. Again, there is nothing wrong with this.

Yet the disconnect that Mike and I now felt with the current group's focus remained. That disconnect boiled down to a single simple question: **Were we showing up to grow each other's businesses, or were we showing up to grow each other?**

SHOW UP TO GROW EACH OTHER

Broadly speaking, a mastermind group is where you show up to grow your business. An Accountability Circle is where you show up to grow each other. And by the way, the very best way to grow your company OVER THE LONG HAUL is to commit yourself fully to growing yourself and others!

A NEW KIND OF GROUP

Let me be clear. There was and is absolutely nothing wrong with a mastermind group taking a transactional, revenue-focused approach. And the people who were in that particular group had every right to focus on short-term income results. They also wanted to focus on networking, which is another common interest of such groups. But Mike and I concluded that we wanted something more—something that a typical mastermind group simply could not provide.

Of course we both wanted to make our business as good as it could be. But we realized that by focusing primarily on the metrics and the bottom line, we would be shortchanging ourselves. All we would be learning would be tactics. There is nothing wrong with tactics, of course, but tactics alone were not going to get us where we wanted to go. What Mike and I needed was a regularly scheduled discussion where we could focus on becoming the very best *people* we could possibly be. We realized that the only way the tactics of our business, or anything else in our lives, could consistently be the very best would be for Mike and me to become *our* very best.

So we left that mastermind group…and we decided to create a new kind of group with each other.

We did know of mastermind groups that transcended tactics and, through the cultivation of trust among the group members, became something more significant. That is what Mike and I wanted to create for ourselves.

THE ACCOUNTABILITY PARTNERSHIP EMERGES

At first, our arrangement was informal. We kept in touch with each other by phone once a week or so, making time to discuss not just what was going on in our businesses, but what was happening in all aspects of our life. Mike had been a good friend of mine for some years, but somehow these phone sessions seemed to bring us even closer. We resolved to feel comfortable saying anything to each other, secure in the knowledge that whatever we said was private. Whenever we had an idea that we felt would help the other person, we considered ourselves obligated to share it. Whenever we spotted something that was keeping the other person from moving forward in the direction he wanted to move, we felt ourselves obliged to mention that as well.

We came to look forward to these calls…and eventually we came to depend on them. Before long, we had taken it to the next level, making a point of scheduling these weekly calls with each other so that we could go over the most important issues we were facing that week in our family lives, in our professional lives, and even in our spiritual lives.

At this point, I need to make something very clear: I could not have had these kinds of discussions with just anyone. Mike was, and is, a special person. I came to understand just how remarkable he was as our weekly calls continued and as I developed an increasingly clearer sense of how committed he was to sharing whatever insights and experiences he had that could help me on my journey. During our calls, I realized that Mike truly has a servant's heart, and I was inspired to follow his example on this front.

But even before I got a clear personal sense of how important it was to Mike that we both grow and develop and help each other to create better lives, I knew that there was something about him that set him apart from other friends. This was a special kind of partnership.

THE THREE CRITICAL TRAITS OF AN ACCOUNTABILITY PARTNER

Specifically, there were three things Mike did that most others in my world did not do. I had identified all three of these factors long before Mike and I started our weekly check-ins. Collectively, they were the reason that I treasured and valued him as a friend. I share them with you now so that you will know what kind of traits you should be looking for as you consider potential members of your own Accountability Circle. Remember, not everyone you know or feel comfortable talking to will be a great fit for your Accountability Circle.

The three traits I am highlighting as mandatory for inclusion in any Accountability Circle have nothing to do with the size of the person's bank account, the job title that is printed on their business card, or the social circles in which they spend their time. These traits have everything to do with the kind of person that individual is committed to being for themselves, for you, and for others.

What I knew for sure about the kind of person Mike was committed to being, long before we agreed to form our special alliance together, was the following:

I knew his word was his bond. This was incredibly important to everything that followed, not least because we had to trust each other implicitly about the confidentiality of the things that we would be sharing with each other in our phone calls and one-on-one meetings. Mike and I agreed to discuss intimate details of our family lives, our relationship issues, and our finances.[1] When Mike and I agreed to keep our conversations private, I did not have to wonder whether or not he meant it. I knew from personal experience that he would not make a commitment and then ignore it. If you are considering recruiting someone for your Accountability Circle and you have even the slightest reason to doubt that person's ability or willingness to keep his or her word, move on to someone else.

---

1   As a side note, I should point out that Mike and I also respect the confidences of other people during our Accountability Circle discussions. We do not identify people who have not given us permission to talk about them.

I knew he walked his talk. I knew that Mike was driven by Values and that his Values were reflected in his life choices. Like a lot of people, Mike says that his family is important. Unlike a lot of people, he supports that stated Value with his choices and actions. One of Mike's busy seasons professionally is August through October. If he wanted to, he could work every single day of those three months and be well rewarded financially for doing so. It is a little like being an accountant. The period leading up to April 15th is just incredibly busy for accountants. That is what it is like for Mike in August, September, and October.

Yet because his family is important to him, he is scrupulously careful about protecting family time during this intensely busy and potentially lucrative time of the year. He built the kids' soccer games and other activities into his schedule. He took a full week off of every month during his business's busiest period of the year to be with his family. That is what it means to walk your talk!

If the person you are considering admitting into your Accountability Circle says that he or she values something, but then does not make decisions that support that Value, move along to someone else. That person does not walk the talk.

I knew he valued and respected everyone with whom he came in contact. Have you ever had the experience of interacting with a total stranger who treated you, for no obvious reason, like your opinions and feelings really mattered—simply because you were a human being? That was how Mike treated people all the time. He had—and has—an inherent respect for the dignity and individuality of everyone in the human family. I admired that trait deeply, and I found myself inspired to follow his example.

Have you ever spent time with someone you thought you admired… and then seen that person treat a customer service associate, waiter, or some other stranger disrespectfully? What did that tell you about how admirable that person really was? Of course, we all have moments of stress, moments when we are not at our best, moments when we do not treat others with the respect they deserve. But I have noticed something interesting about people: some of them regret those moments when they treat others disrespectfully and impatiently because they know that both sides lose a part of themselves in that moment, and so they seek to make amends. Others, in sharp contrast, behave as though it is their birthright to treat people they believe are inferior or subordinate as "less than." When it comes to picking an Accountability Partner, you want to choose someone who falls into the first category.

Now, here is the really interesting thing about Mike. In his case, all three of those positive traits I have mentioned are reflected, and very easy to spot, in what he does for a living. More precisely, making his word his bond, walking his talk, and respecting people *as people* are all essential parts of the *service* that lies at the heart of Mike's life. That is not always the case when you are considering potential Accountability Partners, but it is certainly worth noticing when it *is* the case. Why? Because your Accountability Partner should set an example that makes you want to be a better person! And if the service they render does that, you should take that into account. (We will be discussing that important word *service* in much more depth a little later in the book.)

Mike is a professional public speaker, just like I am. He has a powerful and inspiring message to share—one that is central to his identity, not just as a speaker, but as a human being. You see, years ago, Mike's sister was raped. That is a deep trauma for the person who experiences it…and it is also a trauma for that person's family members. The way Mike responded to that trauma unleashed a powerful and inspiring sense of Purpose that has affected his whole life. He launched The Date Safe Project, which later became the Center for Respect. To quote from their website:

Decades before sexual assault cases were on the cover of every major media publication, Mike Domitrz was being brought in by leading educational institutions, organizations of all sizes, and the U.S. military to help them pursue a new standard of consent and respect… [He is] one of the world's leading influencers and thought-leaders on the topic of respect and consent.

In 2003, Mike founded The Date Safe Project (now The Center for Respect) which conducts training for tens of thousands each year in middle schools, high schools, universities, military installations around the world, and for organizations of all sizes (corporations and associations).

In other words, Mike decided to make a difference. He began researching the sensitive issues of sexual assault and sexual intimacy, and what he found was that most sexual assault seminars were perceived as both boring and ineffective. Mike took it upon himself to create a fun, interactive, and thought-provoking program that would make it easier for people to communicate effectively with others in intimate situations…and keep the tragedy that had happened to his sister from happening to other people.

Mike's life story, and in particular the *service* he has resolved to deliver to others as a result of what he has experienced in life, made me want to be a better person. So it was easy to decide that he belonged in my inner circle. That is where he ended up, and years later, that is where he remains.

WHEN EVALUATING A POTENTIAL ACCOUNTABILITY PARTNER...

...ask yourself:

- Is this person's word their bond?

- Do they have Values they support with actions, not just words?

- Does this person respect and honor the dignity of people?

- Does this person make you want to be a better person?

A HIGH STANDARD

I am describing my own initial system for evaluating anyone I would consider allowing into my inner circle. (And make no mistake, your Accountability Circle is your inner circle!) I am urging you to use the same system for the simple reason that I know it works. I know it will keep you from spinning your wheels with someone who is not really ready to step up on your behalf. Yes, these criteria set a pretty high standard, and they eliminate most casual contacts from consideration. That is intentional.

By the same token, though, I do not want you to think that you are on the lookout for someone who is already "perfect" or that you yourself have to be "perfect" in order to make the ideas in this book work for you. Mike and I will be the first to tell you that we are far from perfect. We are human and therefore fallible. As humans who have learned through failure, we strongly recommend that you start looking closely at how these three simple, powerful standards—your word is your bond; you walk your talk; and you have a big, motivating *Why* that gets you up in the morning—fit into *your* life. Think of them as a two-way street. They have to operate in both directions if you are to get anything at all from your Accountability Circle.

Remember that this is all about interdependence. You are creating a new kind of relationship, a relationship in which everyone agrees that keeping your word, walking your talk, and pursuing your true calling in life are essential to living every single day. We assume that these are truths that can be considered self-evident. Within the Accountability Circle, these three points cannot be debated. Everyone in the Circle *must* be able to count on these truths as shared realities, and if there is, for some reason, a temporary deviation from one or more of them, everyone in the group needs to be able to speak up about that. If you can all count on that much, then you can count on each other, and it is an Accountability Circle. If you cannot count on that much, then you cannot count on each other, and it is not an Accountability Circle.

Will all of you always act in accordance with these three criteria? Probably not, but that is no reason not to try. I would like to say here that my relationship with Mike within our Accountability Circle has certainly helped me feel more confident about my own ability to live a life in which my word is my bond, I walk my talk, and I strive to respect and honor people *as people.*

Which brings us to the *service* that lies at the heart of my life. Since we have looked closely at Mike's service to others, it seems appropriate to look at mine, too. I want to build a more accountable world. I believe you can do that only by helping people be accountable individually. I believe you can do *that* only by building more accountable relationships, and I also believe that when you build more accountable relationships, it is easier to build accountable organizations. Once you build more accountable organizations, I believe you help create more accountable communities. And finally, I believe that building accountability within the community in which you live leads to a more accountable world. I am here for all of that. That is my big *Why*.

What exactly do I mean by "accountable"? How can we get a deeper understanding of that important, often-misused word? Glad you asked. We will examine those questions in the next chapter.

ACCOUNTABILITY TAKEAWAYS: CHAPTER 2

Having a close friend does not mean you have an Accountability Partner.

Mastermind groups and similar gatherings are about showing up to grow the business; an Accountability Circle is all about showing up to grow each other.

Someone you consider taking on as an Accountability Partner should possess the following characteristics:

- Their word is their bond.

- They have Values they support with actions, not just words.

- They respect and honor people simply because they are people.

- They make you want to be a better person.

CHAPTER 3

MOVING BEYOND THE
ACCOUNTABILITY MYTH

EVERYTHING we have been taught about accountability is wrong!

I said that earlier in the book, and yes, I am repeating it here. Why? Because the point warrants repetition. Let me share a true story that will help clarify what I mean when I say this and why it is such an important point.

My Accountability Partner Mike called me a while back very excited and told me that he wanted to be sure that I heard about an interesting exchange he had recently been part of. Mike said it was important that I hear about this particular discussion right away, because I was about to go into an interview for an article in a major national magazine. Mike thought I might be able to use the story in my upcoming interview. I was intrigued. I asked what it was all about. His answer: "Accountability."

Mike had been having a conversation with three CEOs over breakfast at a hotel restaurant, just moments before speaking in front of their association. The word *accountability* happened to come up. One of the executives smiled and said to Mike:

"Listen. I've already got a wife and an executive assistant. Believe me, I don't need any more accountability!"

Mike said that both of the other CEOs laughed at that line. But I have to say, I do not see anything funny about it, and neither did Mike. There is a big problem with what that CEO said. Do you see what it is?

Remember: Accountability is about supporting *relationships* by making and keeping commitments to people. In less than fifteen seconds, this CEO not only insulted his wife and his assistant, but he also denigrated all of his employees. How? By insisting that he has no reason to make, or fulfill, *any* meaningful commitment to *anyone* in his organization. He also proved (at least to me) that he does not deserve even to be called a leader!

This is an incredibly important point. Please take a moment to consider what that CEO is really saying. For this executive, accountability is a way of *doing*, and it is a one-way street. Of course, he still expects others in his organization—specifically, his own direct reports—to be "accountable to" him. Right? He did not say everyone else had enough accountability in their world. Only him!

For his part, he thinks he already has way too much accountability in his life. As a result, he feels he has no need to be "accountable to" anybody else. So for this executive, accountability is not yet a way of *thinking*. For him, accountability is either a stick to be used on other people when he does not get what he wants, or it is a stick to be used against *him* when others do not get what they want. He does not like that second option, but he is fine with the concept of "holding others accountable."

Welcome to the Accountability Myth. This myth boils down to a simple, flawed, and widely accepted idea: **"People being 'accountable to' me is mandatory, but me being 'accountable to' them is optional."**

That is not how accountability works.

THE ACCOUNTABILITY MYTH

When we operate under the assumption that people being "accountable to" me is mandatory, but me being "accountable to" them is optional, we buy into a dangerous misconception.

In the real world, accountability is a two-way street. It does not come about because we demand it from others. It comes about because we are accountable first and we inspire others to follow our example.

The Accountability Myth is false logic. It is the opposite of leadership, because true leadership (in your own life, on a team, or in an organization) is always about accountability for and/or to the people with whom you have relationships.

The Accountability Myth is a proven recipe for underachievement. It destroys relationships, teams, and organizations.

So if that is not how accountability works, what is? To understand what accountability is, you have to start by understanding a critical point that I cannot emphasize enough—namely, that *you are responsible for things...but you are accountable to people.*

A major misconception people have about accountability is that accountability is simply a ball and chain, a means of controlling others, and thus something that they want no part of.

In fact, accountability is commitment. Specifically, accountability is keeping your commitments *to people*. Relationships are what we are really talking about here. Accountability is always—repeat, *always*—based on our (spoken or unspoken) commitments to people, in support of a relationship…and commitments are **no matter what**. They are absolute.

If I simply announce that "I am holding you accountable for doing such-and-such," that means that I am trying to use the word *accountability* to manipulate you to do something I want. I am tearing the relationship down, because I am not leading with my commitments to you.

All too often, when people hear the word *accountable*, what they think is, "Uh-oh. So-and-so is now going to put pressure on me to do something I have not been doing and did not make any commitment to do. But I now have to pretend I am personally committed to doing that, because he or she is in a position of authority."

That is not accountability. That is an order, a mandate, a power trip. If there is no attempt to support the relationship with a commitment, then there is no accountability. It is really as simple as that.

Me giving you an order has nothing to do with accountability. The very phrase "holding you accountable for such-and-such" is an oxymoron. Accountability is not about getting some particular task done. Accountability is not a way of *doing*. Accountability is a way of *thinking*—specifically, a way of thinking about people and relationships.

COMMITMENTS

A true leader—which can be you, me, or anyone and does not require a specific job title (or even any job title)—makes certain meaningful commitments *to people*. Note that these are not tactical commitments, like getting the report done, making the prescribed number of sales calls, or taking out the garbage. These are relational commitments, like the larger commitment to make one's word one's bond!

Do you see the difference? Getting tasks completed that you are assigned to do or volunteer to do is great, but on their own those are quite narrow tactical commitments. The larger commitment to ensure that *all* one's agreements are honored, by contrast, speaks directly to the relationships in our lives. That is what connects them to leadership. Tactical commitments are about things. Relational commitments are about people.

TACTICAL VS. RELATIONAL

Tactical commitments are about things.
Relational commitments are about people.

We will explore in detail what the most important relational commitments are in Chapter 18. For right now, though, just understand that the three traits that set an Accountability Partner apart—our word is our bond, we walk our talk, and we honor and respect people simply because they are people—are the starting point, the foundation, of the most meaningful relational commitments.

Once it becomes clear that our word is our bond...that we make relational commitments based on sound Values and follow through on those commitments no matter what...that we respect people just because they are people... there is the potential for an accountable *relationship*. Not before. All three of those pieces must be in place.

WHAT ACCOUNTABILITY LOOKS LIKE

Accountability *does not* mean, "I just noticed there is a problem, and you did not do anything about it yet."

Accountability *does* mean, "Here is what I am specifically committing to in our relationship…and here is how I am following through on those commitments." *But* notice the kind of commitments I am talking about do not have to be stated in words and in fact may be strongest when they are not stated in words but rather proven by action. My *actions* must convey that I have made a meaningful commitment to you.

WORDS VS. ACTIONS

Our actions must convey that we have made a meaningful commitment to someone. Our words are not as important and may not even be necessary.

Accountability is never punitive. It is never about making people stand up in front of the group and say, "Gosh, I am so sorry. That will not ever happen again." Yes, that kind of response is ownership—it is responsibility. It is positive when there has been a mistake of some kind. But the instinct to *make* someone apologize is *not* accountability. Instead, accountability is always about possibility. Accountability is always positive. Accountability is always inspiring. It does not divide people. If it polarizes a team, a family, or a community, it is not accountability.

Accountability always brings people together. It is always collaborative. And collaborative relationships always outperform adversarial relationships. Collaborative work environments always outperform competitive, adversarial ones.

Accountability is *not* about saying, "I'm holding you accountable." When you say that, it is like putting a gun to the person's head. No one wants to be "held accountable." No one wants to feel coerced.

Instead, accountability is about following through on your own meaningful commitments first...and then helping someone else make and keep meaningful commitments that support the relationship. Accountability is coming alongside someone and helping them be accountable, helping them achieve their goals. This is an entirely different kind of relationship: positive and supportive.

And by the way, there are two different expressions of accountability we must understand and take into account. The first is called *accountability to*. As a child, you are *accountable to* your parents. As an adult, you may be *accountable for* them as they age and you are in charge of paying their bills, keeping them safe, and maintaining their living environment. As an employee, you are *accountable to* your boss. As the CEO of an organization, you are *accountable for* everyone in the company and also *accountable to* them for commitments, spoken or unspoken, like providing a safe space for them to work and telling the truth.[2] If you are *accountable to*, you are not necessarily *accountable for*, but if you are *accountable for* you are always also *accountable to*.

If you are accountable to someone, you are committed to supporting specific relational and tactical commitments to that person.

If you are accountable for someone, you are accountable *to* them... *and* you are personally responsible for some critical aspect of that individual's well-being.

---

2   Providing a safe space and being truthful are implied commitments of any effective leader. They should not have to be spoken out loud.

ACCOUNTABLE TO, ACCOUNTABLE FOR

If you are *accountable to* someone, you are committed to supporting specific relational and tactical commitments to that person.

If you are *accountable for* someone, you are accountable *to* them...*and* you are personally responsible for some critical aspect of that individual's well-being.

In both situations, though, the basic principle remains the same: we are responsible for things, but we are accountable to (and sometimes for) people.

DON'T CONFUSE ACCOUNTABILITY WITH RESPONSIBILITY

Very often, people will talk about "commitments" and "accountability"...when what they really mean to be talking about is "responsibility."

The tactical items on your to-do list are responsibilities, just as the items on your job description are responsibilities. They are not accountabilities, for the simple reason that they are *things* you do, not *people* you serve. Again: we are responsible for things, but we are accountable to people!

The deeper relational commitments you make within an Accountability Circle are not to-do list items or tactical best practices. They are personal priorities that lead to *accountable relationships that support you being the best you that you can possibly be.* Your priorities for those relationships may not ever be spoken out loud to anyone other than your Accountability Circle partners. But they will be there. And notice that here I am talking about relationships within your Accountability Circle, but also about *all* of your relationships.

Why bother with this kind of distinction? Why change from a mindset that says "I am holding you accountable" to one that looks for meaningful commitments that *you* can make and honor? Why invest the time, effort, energy, and attention necessary to contribute to, and benefit from, an Accountability Circle? Why bother taking the initiative? Why bother building accountable relationships?

Because you will make better decisions by doing so. Because you will enjoy the true peace of mind that comes with knowing you are getting the absolute most out of your own potential and helping someone else get the absolute most out of theirs. Because by abandoning the Accountability Myth and by accepting that true accountability is always a two-way street that you travel first, you will set yourself on the path to becoming the person you are truly meant to be.

ACCOUNTABILITY TAKEAWAYS: CHAPTER 3

Accountability is *not* about saying, "I'm holding you account-able." When you say that, it is like putting a gun to the person's head. No one wants to be "held accountable." Instead, accountability is about following through on your own meaningful relational commitments first...and then helping someone else make and keep meaningful commitments that support the relationship.

The Accountability Myth boils down to a simple, flawed, and widely accepted idea: "People being 'accountable to' me is mandatory...but me being 'accountable to' them is optional."

The Accountability Myth is the opposite of leadership, because true leadership (in your own life, on a team, or in an organization) is always about accountability for and/or to the people with whom you have relationships.

Accountability is always—repeat, *always*—based on our (spoken or unspoken) commitments to people, in support of a relationship...and commitments are no matter what. They are absolute.

Once it becomes clear that our word is our bond...that we make commitments based on sound Values and follow through on those commitments no matter what...that we respect people just because they are people, there is the potential for an accountable *relationship.* Not before. All three of those pieces must be in place.

Our actions must convey that we have made a meaningful commitment to someone. Our words are not as important and may not even be necessary. These are not tactical commitments; they are relational commitments!

If you are *accountable to* someone, you are committed to supporting specific relational and tactical commitments to that person.

If you are *accountable for* someone, you are accountable *to* them...*and* you are personally responsible for some critical aspect of that individual's well-being.

CHAPTER 4

THE LADDER OF UNDERSTANDING

MOST PEOPLE I RUN INTO have a deeply flawed understanding of the word *accountability*. They see accountability either as a kind of weapon to get people to do what they want or as a "ball and chain," something that restricts their own freedom. To take part in an Accountability Circle, you must recognize that these are flawed, toxic conceptions of accountability. You have to create a deeper level of understanding.

MOVING BEYOND "I AM HOLDING YOU ACCOUNTABLE"

The kind of understanding we are talking about is a lifelong process...but a broad, foundational understanding of accountability is possible, even essential, for those who are intrigued enough by the ideas I have shared thus far in order to consider what it takes to live a truly accountable life.

There are four rungs on what I call the Ladder of Understanding, which you must climb in order to launch or join an Accountability

Circle. Climbing this ladder means moving upward, from one rung to the next, in our understanding of accountability. It means making a conscious choice to move beyond "holding others accountable" or being "held accountable." This is an essential prerequisite to everything that follows in this book. And I urge you to make that choice.

CLIMB THE LADDER

We can live an accountable life and help others be accountable only by deepening our own understanding of accountability. And that means climbing the Ladder of Understanding.

Each of the four rungs on the Ladder requires the ability to distinguish between two related, but fundamentally different, concepts. Once you have your balance on one rung by being able to recognize the difference between the concepts in question, you will be ready to move up to the next level. All four distinctions are essential if you want a deepened understanding of accountability that goes beyond the common (and toxic) cliché: "I am holding you accountable!"

THE FIRST RUNG

The bottom rung of the Ladder is about understanding the difference between *responsibility* and *accountability*. Yes, I have mentioned this before. Yes, it bears repeating. *We are responsible for things, but we are accountable to people.* If there is accountability, that means there is a commitment from one person to another. Accountability always flows outward from us. We cannot imagine it into existence. It shows up only when we make and follow through on a commitment to another person. This commitment does not have to be stated, and usually the most important and meaningful relational commitments never are.

 Recently, my wife Renee celebrated her birthday. In recognition of the many commitments we have made to each other, both spoken and unspoken, I made a conscious decision to ensure that the day was *not* about the things in my life: the day was about *her*...and *us* as a couple. When I made that decision, and followed through on it by spending the entire day with her, I made a conscious choice to support our relationship by setting aside, for a time, all the things I was *responsible for* so that I could focus on the person I was *accountable for and to*. Life never stops. There is an unending list of things we are *responsible for,* and like just about everyone else, I sometimes get distracted by that list, at the expense of the important relationships in my life. There is a much shorter list of people we are *accountable for and/or to*. This first rung of the Ladder reminds us not to confuse those two lists.

Responsibility
or
Accountability?

THE SECOND RUNG

The second rung of the Ladder is about understanding the difference between *doing* and *thinking*. This distinction, too, bears repeating. Accountability is not a way of doing. It is not about individual activities we can check off our to-do list. Nor is it about what we want other people to do. Accountability is about how we *think* about people and relationships. Accountability is about whether we are willing to *evaluate* our activities through the lens of our connections to others. It is about understanding the impact of our actions (or inactions) on other people. It is about how we *think* about relationships.

Doing or
Thinking?

Responsibility
or
Accountability?

 To return to my example about my day with Renee, I did not make the mistake of treating her birthday like a to-do list item that I needed to check off. I made a conscious, purposeful choice to *think about her* and about our relationship. I was asking questions about how I could improve our connection. What could I do to show her that I supported her? That I cared about her? That I valued and appreciated her? That I was committed to helping her be her best, get the most she possibly could out of life, and find her highest calling? Notice that when we are *doing* activities, we generally assume that we already have all the answers. When we are *thinking* about our relationships to other people, we are asking good questions and *looking* for the answers! We are not assuming that we already know everything there is to know.

THE THIRD RUNG

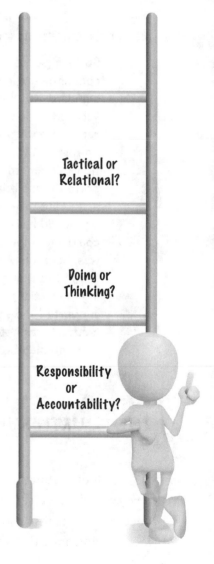

Tactical or Relational?

Doing or Thinking?

Responsibility or Accountability?

The third rung is about understanding the difference between *tactical commitments* and *relational commitments*. A tactical commitment is focused on a particular goal or set of goals. These activities describe the tactics we employ in our lives, our careers, and our businesses. Tactics are important, but they are not everything. They are not the commitments we make to support our relationships. You will be learning a lot more about relational commitments later on in this book. For now, just understand that there is nothing wrong with being goal-oriented, as long as you are people-oriented at the same time. The commitments that build accountability are never the tactical commitments.

They are always relational commitments. And *relational commitments are always people-oriented!*

The problem comes when we prioritize tasks over people, when we get so distracted with the *how* that we lose sight of the *why*. Relational commitments help us keep our priorities straight. Responsibility connects to the tactics, but accountability always flows from the relational commitments we make.

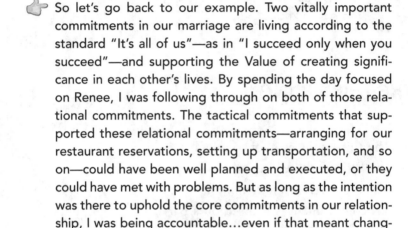 So let's go back to our example. Two vitally important commitments in our marriage are living according to the standard "It's all of us"—as in "I succeed only when you succeed"—and supporting the Value of creating significance in each other's lives. By spending the day focused on Renee, I was following through on both of those relational commitments. The tactical commitments that supported these relational commitments—arranging for our restaurant reservations, setting up transportation, and so on—could have been well planned and executed, or they could have met with problems. But as long as the intention was there to uphold the core commitments in our relationship, I was being accountable...even if that meant changing the tactics along the way. The specific tasks of that day supported the specific relational commitments that I had made. It was not implementing the tactics that made me accountable; it was fulfilling the relational commitments.

THE FOURTH RUNG

The fourth rung is about understanding the difference between *physical* and *spiritual*. Our activities and our tactics are going to produce certain results, also known as outcomes. We usually choose to focus on outcomes that are countable and measurable. If we can touch

something with our hands, if we can mea-
sure it, we believe that it is real, or at least
relevant to our world. There is nothing
wrong with this way of looking at things.
This viewpoint allows us to take stock of
our stuff: our house, our car, our annual
bonus, our company's profits for the year,
whatever. Stuff is important; stuff is part of
life, and we cannot ignore it. But you know
what? "Stuff" is not everything. And it is
not our "stuff" that brings us ultimate hap-
piness and satisfaction.

At some point, we also need to ask ourselves: *Why are we here? What is our Purpose with a capital P? Are we fulfilling that
Purpose?* These are questions worth considering at some length. Each of us must
identify our own Purpose in this life. If we
look closely enough for our own unique
Purpose, I believe we will ultimately realize that no matter how personal the Purpose we discover may be to our own life
and experience, it can always be found
within the borders of a single, essential
word: *service.*

How are we *serving* the rest of the
human family? This is a spiritual question,
one we can apply to any and every situation. And accountability is not complete
without it. Do not misunderstand that
word *spiritual*—this has nothing to do

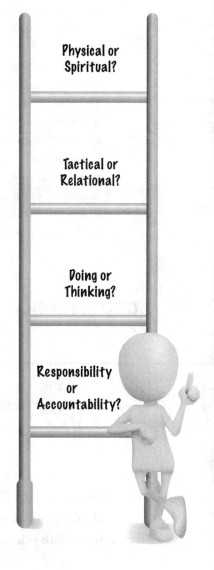

**Physical or
Spiritual?**

**Tactical or
Relational?**

**Doing or
Thinking?**

**Responsibility
or
Accountability?**

with religion and everything to do with what *inspires* us to improve the quality and depth of our relationships.

 This rung of the Ladder is all about *service*. At the fourth level of understanding, my service to Renee during our day together had to take the form of *focused presence and authentic personal attention*. (I like to think that it did, but ultimately Renee has to be the judge of that.) The only way I could possibly be of service to her, or to the relationship, during that special day was to be fully, personally engaged in it as it played out. "Just showing up" is physical. Really being there—meaning, showing up with the intention of being in service to the relationship—is spiritual, and it connects to my larger Purpose in life. If I had delegated the task of taking Renee out to a restaurant to my assistant, I would have been making sure that the food got eaten...but I would not have been present for the relationship, and I would not have been serving it in a spiritual or personal sense.

ACCOUNTABILITY IS INSPIRING

Accountability, understood by means of the four rungs on this Ladder, is inspiring. It connects us powerfully to other people and indeed to the larger human family. It gives us a deep sense of Purpose, the incredible feeling that we are doing what we were meant to do with our lives.

Unlike the false version of "accountability" people appeal to when they say things like "I am holding you accountable," true accountability expresses itself only in the desire to improve our relationships with others...by becoming a better person.

Ultimately, accountability is all about becoming the person we were meant to be. The only way I can possibly become a better person is by making my relationships with other people better! And this is why we take part in an Accountability Circle: to improve our own lives by improving our relationships with others.

Notice that the four distinctions I have shared with you in the Ladder of Understanding are *complementary*, not sequential. They all unfold at the same time. Let me give you a business example of how the four distinctions on the Ladder of Understanding play out in an accountable workplace so you can see how they connect to one another in a different environment.

> Let's say you lead a team. What does the first rung look like? Your *responsibilities* might show up in your job description, but your *accountabilities* are always going to show up in your relationships with people. *Real leaders focus on the relationship first!*

> How about the second rung? If we are a truly accountable leader, we are not going to fixate on the ways we can manipulate our people to *do* more. We are going to place a priority on *thinking* about our relationships with our people in such a way as to put *our relational commitments to them* at the forefront. Do we see our people as having potential? As being able to solve problems? If we are not thinking about our workplace relationships that way, we are managing...not leading.

> On the third rung, we have to ask ourselves a tough question: Are we focused only on whether our people are accumulating checkmarks and completing the processes we have laid out for them...or are we also focused on *our* specific relational commitments to *them*? If we know what our relational commitments to our team members are and we are keeping those commitments, regardless of

whether those commitments are spoken or unspoken, we are pursuing the path of accountable leadership.

 Finally, on the fourth rung, are we focused totally on outcomes, on metrics, on *stuff*...or are we focused on *service* to the team, the organization, and the larger world? Do we connect what we are doing all day long to our larger Purpose in life? Here I would point out that traditional leadership is focused on *tasks*, while accountable leadership is focused on something very different: serving the people with whom they have relationships. This, I believe, is the difference between a manager and a leader. Managers focus all their energy and attention on task-based outcomes, on countable results, while leaders focus on the *service* that supports relational outcomes...and let their people focus on the tasks.

ACCOUNTABILITY TAKEAWAYS: CHAPTER 4

We can live an accountable life and help others be accountable only by deepening our own understanding of accountability. And that means climbing the Ladder of Understanding.

There is a difference between responsibility and accountability. We are responsible for things. We are accountable to people.

There is a difference between doing and thinking. Accountability is not a way of doing. It is a way of thinking about our relationships.

There is a difference between tactical commitments and relational commitments. A tactical commitment is an activity that is focused on a particular goal or set of goals. Relational commitments are always people-oriented.

There is a difference between the physical and the spiritual. We usually choose to focus on outcomes that are countable and measurable—the physical "stuff" of our world. Stuff is not everything! We also have to look at the spiritual side, which means we have to identify our Purpose with a capital P. Our unique Purpose will always be found within the borders of a single, essential word: *service*.

CHAPTER 5

THE TEN AGREEMENTS
OF THE
ACCOUNTABILITY CIRCLE

WHEN WE ARE part of an Accountability Circle, we agree to live by ten critical principles in all our interactions with those who share the Circle with us. These principles are *agreements* without which the Circle cannot function. Just as a building loses its structural integrity if we take away a critical pillar, so an Accountability Circle loses its functional integrity if we lose sight of these agreements, pretend we have not made them, or act as though they do not exist.

 We agree that self-accountability makes accountability to others possible. We show up with the intention of establishing full congruence in our lives between what we say we are committed to and what we are committed to in practice. We acknowledge that we cannot give what we do not have. We understand that in order to win the right to speak into someone else's life and shape someone else's choices, we must honor certain relational commitments in our own life first—and important among these are *making our word our bond, walking our talk,* and *respecting people simply because they are people.* We accept that if we are not doing these things, there is no reason for anyone within the Circle (or outside of it) to want to hear what we have to say. It is only when we are working to be accountable and live these important commitments that other people in our lives will be inspired to do the same.

 We agree that peer relationships matter. This means we interact as equals and accept that no one in the Circle carries any more weight than anyone else. My voice is no more powerful than yours. I am no more right than you are. Just because I think something does not make it right. We are equals in this relationship, no matter how long we have been part of the Accountability Circle.

 We agree to live by our stated Values, and if we do not have them yet, we agree to take the time to create them in writing. You will be learning more about how to write Personal Value Narratives in the second section of this book. For now, just understand this: We can say that X is a Value of ours, but until we defend X in the moment of having to make a difficult decision, then there is no proof that X really is one of our core Values. When there is proof in our actions of what we believe, and when other people see clarity in our mind and heart, that defines what we believe, even when it is not popular or easy to stand up for it, other people want to be in our orbit. In an Accountability Circle, we *choose* to be in each other's orbit, based on the Values that guide our lives. That means I have to know exactly what you stand for, and I have to see clear evidence that you really do stand for it, in order for me to trust your voice in shaping the decisions I am making in my own life.

 We agree to speak up when we notice someone in the Circle whose actions do not align with their stated Values (including ourselves). We all make mistakes. We walk in the door admitting that we are not perfect, that we need to grow and learn and become better people. If I cannot count on you to help me do that, then I am not getting everything I should be getting from the discussion. By the same token, if I do not speak up to help you when you need help, then I am letting you down. If we saw a toddler walking toward a busy traffic intersection, we would not ask ourselves whether it was our place to rush over and pick her up—we would just do it. When someone speaks up to help us within the Accountability Circle, we assume good intent. We do not get defensive or antagonistic. We interact with each other with compassion.

We agree to celebrate each other's successes and achievements. This is vitally important. Every success is worth celebrating. Small successes are just as essential to celebrate as big ones.

We agree to share only relevant insights and expertise. If sharing our own experience supports someone in the Circle, we share it. If that kind of sharing is not helpful, we do not share it. We never give feedback simply to be heard, to make ourselves feel good, to prove how smart we are, or to prove how right we are. We recognize that upholding this agreement takes practice and dedication.

We agree to seek input, share everything, hide nothing, and ask only pertinent questions. We give open, honest, and respectful full disclosure. We agree that everything is on the table. We do not pretend that accountability applies to some areas of our lives, but not others. We do not waste precious time.

We agree that this is a work in process for everyone in the Circle. I want to be better, not perfect. I want everyone in the Circle to be better together. I understand that this is a continual, never-ending journey in search of my new best self, and that everyone else in the Accountability Circle is on that same journey. What counts is not the destination but the shared commitment to the journey.

We agree to keep this a safe space. We talk about behaviors and decisions, not people. We do not make personal attacks. We respect confidence. Specifically, we do not share the details of our conversations with outsiders without permission. There are no exceptions to this. Without this agreement to respect confidentiality, we cannot create a safe space. We speak up when necessary on behalf of the Circle.

 We agree to answer the Three Big Questions on an ongoing basis in our own life and help the members of the Circle answer them on an ongoing basis in their lives.[3]

The Three Big Questions are:

 What do I believe? If we do not know what we believe and are unwilling to compromise on, we are not going to make consistently good decisions. (For instance: "I believe in keeping commitments." And: "I believe in living by the Golden Rule.") If we do not yet know what we believe, we need to find out! Note that it is our actions that show us and everyone around us exactly what we believe—not our words.

 What do I focus on? We must focus on what we can control, not on what we cannot control. When we focus on what we cannot control, we make excuses; when we focus on what we can control, we make decisions and get results.

 What do I commit to? Within the Circle, we are explicit in our commitments. We understand the distinction between tactical commitments and relational commitments: tactical commitments are about things; relational commitments are about people.

---

3   To learn more about the transformative power of the Three Big Questions, check out the Sam's book *Pivot!*, which is available at: http://samsilverstein.com/shop.

All of these agreements are important, but I want to place particular emphasis on the tenth item on this list. The Three Big Questions will change your life. They will help you and everyone in your Circle stay on track and remain accountable. Consider: There are all kinds of things in this life that we cannot control. But we *can* control our belief system, what we pay attention to (and how we react to what we pay attention to), and what we commit to. The Three Big Questions put you in the driver's seat of your own life, which is where you belong.

You now have a comprehensive overview of accountability, an understanding of the agreements that make an Accountability Circle possible, and a much clearer sense of why what most of us have been taught to believe about accountability is wrong. In the next part of the book, you will begin looking at the concepts of personal Purpose, personal Mission, and personal core Values that make commitment-driven conversations in an Accountability Circle possible.

ACCOUNTABILITY TAKEAWAYS: CHAPTER 5

The Ten Agreements of an Accountability Circle are:

1. We agree that self-accountability makes accountability to others possible.

2. We agree that peer relationships matter.

3. We agree to live by our stated Values, and if we do not have them yet, we agree to take the time to create them in writing.

4. We agree to speak up when we notice someone in the Circle whose actions do not align with their stated Values (including ourselves).

5. We agree to celebrate each other's successes and achievements.

6. We agree to share only relevant insights and expertise.

7. We agree to seek input, share everything, hide nothing, and ask only pertinent questions.

8. We agree that this is a work in process for everyone in the Circle.

9. We agree to keep this a safe space.

10. We agree to answer the Three Big Questions on an ongoing basis in our own life and help the members of the Circle answer them on an ongoing basis in their lives.

   - What do I believe?

   - What do I focus on?

   - What do I commit to?

PART II

PURPOSE, MISSION, AND VALUES

CHAPTER 6

ACCOUNTABILITY
AND PURPOSE

AN ACCOUNTABILITY CIRCLE is all about making and keeping relational commitments to other people.

What drives those commitments, clarifies them, supports them, and turns them into realities? Three things: our **Purpose**, our **Mission**, and our **Values**. They are frequently confused with one another, frequently mislabeled, and only rarely understood on a practical level. We are going to look closely at them in this second section of the book so that you can finally have the clarity you need. Discovering my Purpose, Mission, and Values has been huge for me. It has brought clarity, focus, and a true sense of the direction in which I should be moving in my life.

Once we get clear on our big *Why*, on the true Purpose of our life, and on the principle of *service* that supports that Purpose, everything else falls into place—specifically, our big *What*, meaning the Mission we undertake, and our big *How*, meaning the rules we play by. And once we are clear on those three things, our lives become easier. These three essential things—Purpose, Mission, and Values—are essential prerequisites to an accountable life and to any meaningful connection and personal growth that may take place within an Accountability Circle.

We cannot be our best without doing the work necessary to figure out what these three things are, and we cannot help others be their best unless they do the work and they know what their Purpose, Mission, and Values are.

WHY PURPOSE, MISSION, AND VALUES MATTER

Being an accountable person means making and keeping meaningful relational commitments, and making meaningful relational commitments means taking the time to clarify your personal Purpose, your personal Mission, and your personal Values. You cannot be your best without doing the work necessary to figure out what those three things are for you.

"WHO AM I?"

Everything that follows about Purpose in this chapter, as well as the four chapters after it, connects to critical, transformative work that is essential to our sense of self and our ability to make and keep relational commitments. Gaining clarity about our Purpose in life is a hallmark of our growth and development as individuals, *whether or not we are in an Accountability Circle.*

Let's get to work!

Your *Purpose* is the reason you are here, phrased in the form of *service* that you render to others. Your purpose is your *why.*

PURPOSE

 Your *Purpose* is the reason you are here, phrased in the form of *service* that you render to others. Your purpose is your *Why.*

Your Purpose is the answer to the question "Who am I?" It is *compelling*. Once you see your Purpose clearly, once you release yourself to it, the deepest part of you knows that you should support that Purpose with your own "blood, toil, tears, and sweat," to quote the great British prime minister Winston Churchill. Once you release yourself to your Purpose, a little voice inside you says, "This is who I really am. I have to take action on this. I have no alternative."

Paradoxically, though, there is another little voice that pops up, too—a voice that looks for reasons *not* to take action. **This is the voice of your excuses. Once you learn to notice and recognize that voice, you can make better choices about whether you want to focus your attention on it.**

Both voices are in play in all of us, and both are important to recognize. Accountable people are not only aware of what it feels like when they are aligning with their Purpose; they are also aware that excuses are likely to present themselves as good reasons for not taking action on that Purpose. These two awarenesses go hand in hand, and strengthening them is one of the major advantages of taking part in an Accountability Circle.

Committing your Purpose to writing, using words that capture exactly what is compelling *to you* about your Purpose, and sharing that language with your Accountability Partners are all essential steps for moving past the excuses that arise. Creating this kind of language and this kind of awareness may seem to be a challenging task, because locating the words that capture who you really are, what is really non-negotiable to you, and what you are *always* ready to take action on requires a certain amount of effort and self-examination.

BIGGER THAN YOU

Your Purpose is, by definition, both unique to who you are as an individual…and bigger than you. That is the source of its incredible power. It summons you to become something larger and fuller than who you are right now. It forces you to take action, and in so doing, it forces you to grow as a person. It is a limitless source of energy. It does not shift when things around you shift. It is always waiting there for you, whether you feel like recognizing it or not. When you are "On Purpose," you always feel as though you are grounded, no matter the adversity you may be facing. When you are not "On Purpose," you always have the option of finding a way back to that feeling of being grounded. Your Accountability Partners are there to help you with this, and vice versa. In order for an Accountability Circle to function, I have to know what my Purpose is, and I have to know what yours is too!

Releasing yourself to your Purpose is always a truly powerful moment in your life. This experience leads you to a sense of deep calm and peace, even in the midst of difficulty. This is because your Purpose aligns with your true self. When you are operating from your Purpose, you are guided by a deep sense of certainty about what you are supposed to be doing, and you are truly effective as you do it. You are focused on what you can control.

To be sure, releasing yourself to your Purpose can also be scary at first, because it means giving up familiar patterns of behavior that are Off Purpose. But experiencing that fear and taking action anyway is where the power to fulfill your own potential comes in. The experience of being On Purpose is about leveraging that power and reaching the place where you do your very best work.

What takes you out of this extraordinary state of being? You already know. Excuses. But you can always notice what has happened to take you Off Purpose…and you can always release yourself to your Purpose once again.

ON PURPOSE, OFF PURPOSE

 When we take refuge in an excuse that causes us to lose sight of our Purpose, all that means is we have lost sight, temporarily, of what we can control, who we really are, and what we really need to be doing. We are "Off Purpose" at that moment.

A written Declaration of Purpose will help us claim our Purpose as the DRIVING FORCE in our life. And it will speed up the process by which we release ourselves *from* our excuses…and release ourselves *to* our Purpose…so we can stay On Purpose.

We do not beat ourselves up because we have noticed that we have momentarily drifted Off Purpose. That momentary drifting is called being human. The problem would be if we did not take steps to get back On Purpose once we noticed that we had drifted off course. As accountable people, we are constantly correcting our course. Let me share an example with you of what this kind of course correction looks like in action, using a Hollywood narrative with which I suspect you are already familiar.

RELEASING YOURSELF TO YOUR PURPOSE: A LESSON FROM *JAWS*

If you have ever seen the movie *Jaws,* you will recall the astonishing moment when the hero of the story, Martin Brody (played by Roy Scheider), the chief of police in a small Massachusetts seacoast town, releases himself to his Purpose. It is the moment when he releases himself *from* his excuses—and recaptures the Purpose he has momentarily lost sight of. This moment is not only one of the greatest moments in cinema history, but it is also an important object lesson in accountability. Let me set it up for you.

Chief Brody, you will recall from the film, has closed the beaches after the partial remains of a young woman are found on shore. *In taking that action, he is On Purpose.*

How do we know that? Because Brody's Purpose is simple: **to protect people.** He knows in his heart that closing the beaches is the right thing to do. He has every reason to believe the dead woman was the victim of a shark attack. So he acts on his Purpose by ordering the beach to be closed and putting up signs warning people to stay out of the water.

Unfortunately, there is a setback. Political pressures from the mayor of the town, who is eager to ensure that local businesses have a profitable tourist season, cause the town's medical examiner to reverse his initial ruling that the death was due to a shark attack. The coroner backs up the absurd theory that the dismembered body found on the shore was the result of a boating accident. Brody watches helplessly as the mayor reverses the order to close the beaches.

In so doing, Brody buys into an excuse, one that I have bought into myself: "There is nothing I can do." Maybe you have bought into that excuse at some point, too.

It is easy to understand why Brody buys into this excuse. The mayor is his boss. We have all, at one point or another, taken refuge in the idea that the boss cannot be challenged. What I want you to notice now is that the moment Brody accepts the excuse that "There is nothing I can do," he is Off Purpose. He is focusing on what he cannot change and not what is under his control.

At that moment, he has lost sight of who he is and what he has to do. He *knows* what the right thing to do is, but he has found a reason— an excuse—not to do it. The excuse sounds plausible. I do not know whether you identify with that situation, but I certainly do.

Then comes the unforgettable moment when Brody gets back On Purpose.

He is sitting on the beach, staring out at dozens of people playing in and around the water. Suddenly he realizes that he is witnessing a shark attack. Brody stays seated, but somehow his increasingly terrified face seems to get closer and closer to the camera…at the same moment everything behind him starts fading into a blurry obscurity. At that moment, Brody's Purpose becomes utterly clear to him—and to us. All the excuses vanish. He has to **protect people. That is his Purpose!**

Chief Brody no longer pays any attention to the excuse that "There is nothing I can do." He has released himself to his Purpose. Protecting the people in the community is *who he is* for the rest of the movie. That Purpose is what he has to take action on, no matter what. From that moment forward, the film is about one thing and one thing only: Brody taking action on his Purpose.

Look at it again. Brody's Purpose is to **protect people**. Of course he has to do that as the chief of police of Amity Island, Massachusetts… but notice that if he happened to be vacationing in London, England, and he was witnessing a robbery instead of a shark attack, he would still have the same Purpose. *But whether or not he is On Purpose or Off*

Purpose at any given moment depends on whether or not he has bought into an excuse at that moment.

EXCUSES COST US

Excuses are expensive. If we are Off Purpose, it is because we have bought into an excuse. That is too high a price to pay.

THE "DOLLY ZOOM MOMENT"

Back to the movie. That extraordinary cinema shot in which Chief Brody realizes what is happening out on the water takes all of three seconds, but it is really the heart of the film. Here is why: it is the moment when Brody releases himself *from* his excuses and fully releases himself *to* his Purpose.

In those three seconds, we in the audience become emotionally invested in whether Brody gets what he is after…because we see that *he* is totally emotionally invested in his Purpose. He is *present* to his Purpose. When we are present to our Purpose, there are no more excuses! We take action on it!

NO MORE EXCUSES

When we are present to our Purpose, there are no more excuses! We take action on it!

Right after that shot, Brody leaps up and runs to the water's edge. That is the first of many *actions* he takes once he decides that he has no choice *but* to set aside all excuses…and act decisively to protect the people in his community.

Your true Purpose is a driving force. It is *who you really are*. Who you are is *defined* by the actions you take in support of your Purpose. The question is, are you present to your Purpose…or in denial of it? Are you living that Purpose…or making excuses that allow you to justify inaction? Are you On Purpose…or Off Purpose?

By the way, the technical name for the shot Steven Spielberg used to make that astonishing moment in *Jaws* happen is a "dolly zoom." This simply means using the lens to zoom in on the actor's face at the same time the camera is physically moving—dollying—away from the actor on a mechanical track. The result: an instant of extraordinary, intense focus that a traditional close-up simply cannot achieve. Alfred Hitchcock came up with the breakthrough technique; Spielberg learned from the best.

Make no mistake—your written Declaration of Purpose must serve a very similar function. It must allow you to *zoom in* on who you really are and what you really need to do…at the same time that you push your mental camera *away* from your excuses and everything that does not support that Purpose. This brings you an overwhelming focus on what you can control and on what matters most in your life.

You must create a compelling Statement of Purpose that gives you a "dolly zoom" moment, a moment of total release to your unique Purpose. I call this the Moment of Presence.

THE MOMENT OF PRESENCE

This Moment of Presence is crucial because it not only releases you *to* your Purpose, but it also releases you *from* any excuses that are keeping you Off Purpose. And a clear, present-tense engagement with your own Purpose is essential, because this presence is what makes meaningful relational commitments—and accountability itself—possible.

Right now, as you read these words, your Purpose is waiting for you. If you have not yet articulated it, your next big job is to take on the goal of putting your Purpose into words. There are two reasons to do this. First and foremost, clarifying your Purpose makes it less likely that you will lose sight of it and waste any more of your precious time Off Purpose. And second, because participation in an Accountability Circle without a clearly articulated sense of your own Purpose is a waste of your time and everyone else's.

Each of us has our own *Why*. Each of us has our own unique Purpose. Our purpose should drive everything we do as we move through our day and through our life, seeking to live that Purpose fully. And each of us has the opportunity to articulate that Purpose in such a way that it inspires us and moves us to decide "NO MORE EXCUSES" and take action, just like Roy Scheider's character was motivated to cast his excuses aside and take action by going directly to the beach where people were in danger.

It helps to have a single, powerful sentence that instantly reminds you of who you really are and what you need to do right now. Solely by way of example, my Purpose is:

To help people discover their potential and be the best they can possibly be.

We will talk in just a moment about the length and nature of the journey that leads us to the crafting of such a personal Statement of Purpose. For now, just understand that it took time, energy, and focus to articulate that Purpose in a way that made immediate, intuitive, and compelling sense to me, but once I did articulate it, I recognized that that Purpose had been the central part of who I am for my entire adult life. I also recognized that I had in that written Statement of Purpose a powerful tool I could use to create a Moment of Presence for myself any time I needed it.

Now, whenever I read that sentence, I wake up to my Purpose, just as Chief Brody woke up to his in that terrifying moment on the beach. That is as it should be. It is much better to have a sheet of paper that wakes you up. It should not take a disaster to wake you up to your Purpose!

My Purpose, like Chief Brody's, like yours, shows up in *action*. It shows up when I write authentically, when I speak authentically, and when I interact authentically with the people around me. When I make decisions and connect to people in a manner that honors my Purpose, those are actions, too. My Purpose shows up in actions I take to support relationships with my family, my friends, my professional network, and even with people I meet randomly in a store or restaurant. It is who I am…when I take action to support it.

You will know your Purpose when you set it down in words, because you will feel inspired to take action. At a deep personal level, you will sense that this is your most constructive driving force, and you will know in your heart that there is no excuse that justifies ignoring it or failing to put it to use. Your Purpose is the central part of who you are right now, whether you have articulated it or not, and it is asking you to take action.

The challenge that we all face is that our Purpose really is right there, in the middle of our lives, but sometimes we do not recognize that because we have not released ourselves to it.

RECOGNIZING PURPOSE TAKES PRACTICE

 Our Purpose is always right there, at the center of who we are...but we do not always *recognize* that it is there.

Why not? Again, you already know the answer: because our excuses sound so convincing to us! Sometimes we may not even realize when we are making decisions that do not align with our Purpose. Understanding this point means we can understand the best *definition* of an excuse: it is a story we tell ourselves to sell ourselves and to try to sell others.

THE DEFINITION OF AN EXCUSE

 An excuse is a story we tell ourselves to sell ourselves and to try to sell others.

Remember: Before his "dolly zoom" moment, Roy Scheider's character made an excuse. He decided to accommodate someone whose Purpose did not align with his—the mayor of the town—who happened to be his boss and whose main goal was to keep the beach open and have a strong tourist season. He told himself, "There is nothing I can do." He focused on what he thought he could not change. That was a story he told himself and tried to sell to others. After his "dolly zoom" moment, Scheider knows he cannot make that same excuse again, or any excuse, without losing sight of who he really is. And he does not.

The decisions we make when we are Off Purpose do not feel right to us at a gut level. We know we are not achieving the results we seek, even though we may not be able to articulate why that is. **The reason those decisions do not feel right and the outcomes do not satisfy us is that our actions are not aligning with our Purpose. They are aligning with our excuses.**

Once we finally understand our Purpose, release ourselves to it, and release ourselves from excuses, we start making decisions that align with our Purpose...no matter the consequences. We take action, *even if the mayor does not want us to* and *even if it means having a bad tourist season* (to return to our *Jaws* example). That is when we start achieving at our full potential, having the greatest positive impact, and creating the most meaningful relationships. That is when we are who we are meant to be.

WHY FOCUS ON PURPOSE FIRST?

Some people will try to tell you that you should figure out *What* you are doing first and that you should work out the *Why* and the *How* after that. This is a fallacy. The problem with that approach is that it does not do anything to ensure your decision-making aligns with who you really are (or, in the case of a business, why the business exists). This is not a project. This is your life. Once you fully understand the *Why* of your life, that is going to help reveal the *What* and the *How*.

Notice that in the moments right after his "dolly zoom" moment, Roy Scheider's character in *Jaws* knew that he was facing a problem that was *bigger than his own capabilities*...a challenge that he did not know how to resolve on his own. He took action anyway to fulfill a Mission that aligned with his Purpose. We will be talking a lot more about Mission in a later chapter, and we will also look at how Chief Brody takes on his Mission.

For now, though, we are focusing on your Purpose: that which motivates you in both the short term and the long term, that which clarifies *who you really are*. In the next chapter, we will take a much closer look at what may be keeping you from feeling that sense of deep certainty about who you are and why you are here: your own big excuse.

ACCOUNTABILITY TAKEAWAYS: CHAPTER 6

An excuse is a story we tell ourselves to sell ourselves and to try to sell others.

When our decisions do not feel right and the outcomes of those decisions do not satisfy us, that is because our decisions align with our excuses, not our Purpose.

Excuses are expensive. If we are Off Purpose, it is because we have bought into an excuse. That is too high a price to pay.

Our Purpose is always right there, at the center of who we are...but we do not always *recognize* that it is there.

We must create a compelling Statement of Purpose that gives us a "dolly zoom" moment, a moment of total release to our unique Purpose, whenever we need to move past an excuse.

CHAPTER 7

WHAT IS
YOUR **BIG EXCUSE?**

OVER AND OVER AGAIN, we waste our precious time. We find reasons NOT to release ourselves to our Purpose. Why does that happen?

The answer, as I have already suggested, can be found in a single, devastating word: *excuses.*

We *stop* making decisions that align with our Purpose and instead, we make excuses. For Chief Brody, as we discovered last chapter, the excuse sounded like this: "There is nothing I can do." Of course, that was not even close to true, but it sounded convincing enough in the heat of the moment to take him Off Purpose.

"There is nothing I can do" is one of the classic excuses—perhaps the most popular one of all. Other persuasive, powerful excuses that take us Off Purpose include:

👉 "I am too busy right now. I will get to it later."

👉 "I am too old."

👉 "I am too young."

👉 "I am sick."

👉 "I am not good enough."

👉 "This is all I am qualified to do."

👉 "I don't have the support to do what is right."

👉 "It is not the right time."

👉 "I don't know enough."

👉 "I don't have the necessary experience."

👉 "People must (respect me/pay attention to me/acknowledge me/whatever) before I take action in this situation."

👉 And so on.

You get the idea. It is these kinds of excuses that keep us from releasing ourselves to our Purpose. We convince ourselves that they are not only valid in the moment, but *real*, just as Chief Brody convinced himself that "There is nothing I can do" was a valid and real response to the challenge of a shark attack.

The difficult truth with which all of us must eventually come to terms is that in addition to releasing ourselves to our Purpose, we must also find a way to release ourselves *from* our excuses. Our interactions with the people in our Accountability Circle are a critical part of that process. If we become familiar with our own most popular excuses, if we share those excuses with our Accountability Partners, and if they do the same with us, we are all less likely to waste our time being Off Purpose.

All of us have numerous excuses for not releasing ourselves to our Purpose, many of them rooted in our early childhood. In my experience, most of us have one *big* excuse that always seems to materialize when we are about to take action on our Purpose. It is our job to identify this big excuse for what it is—a story that we keep selling ourselves and trying to sell to others—and acknowledge it as such, right out loud, within our Accountability Circle. That is not only so that we can recognize it, but so that our Accountability Partners can recognize it as the excuse that it is, call us on it, and help us move past it!

One of the key integrities of the Accountability Circle is listening to our Accountability Partners when they point out that we are letting an excuse stand in the way of us releasing ourselves to our Purpose. Each of us has a big excuse, an excuse that we buy into more often than any other. We need to understand what this excuse is so we can recognize it. Here, for the record, is my big excuse:

"I cannot show my weaknesses."

When I buy into this excuse, it keeps me from being transparent, learning from situations, opening up, and connecting with other people and expressing empathy to them. It puts barriers between me and those I could be helping and those who could be helping me. It keeps me from getting the resources and support I need to improve. When I avoid admitting to myself or someone else that I do not have all the answers, I am buying into my big excuse.

When my Accountability Partners notice me indulging this excuse in a large or small way, they have a commitment to call me on it...and I have a commitment to them to listen to them and be coachable. By the same token, when I notice a big excuse of theirs surfacing, I have a commitment to share what I have noticed with them.

WHERE EXCUSES COME FROM

Many of our excuses are rooted in a faulty or limited sense of our Purpose in life. Let me share an extremely important piece of advice that will help you release yourself from excuses: *do not confuse your compelling Purpose with the supporting activities that allow you to pursue that Purpose.*

Sometimes I will say to a person with whom I am working, "Tell me what your Purpose in life is. Tell me what the driving force that moves you forward at any and every moment of the day is." You know what I will hear in reply? Something like the following: "My Purpose is to be the highest-paid person in my company." Or, if I am talking to a CEO, I may hear something like this: "Our Purpose as a company is to make 200 million dollars in profit this year." Or: "Our Purpose is to be the number one supplier of widgets to the world." None of those things is a Purpose! They are actually goals—and distractions from your true Purpose. And if you create a story that justifies doing something that you know is wrong because you think doing that is the only way to become the highest-paid person in the company, that story is an excuse. One particularly powerful excuse along these lines is, "At this level, everyone does this kind of thing." or: "If we are going to make our numbers this quarter, then we are going to have to look the other way when such-and-such happens, just this once." Do not buy into that way of thinking!

Look at it this way. We have to breathe to live, right? If we stop breathing, we stop living. So breathing is something we must do. It is critical. *But breathing is not our Purpose. Breathing is something we do in order to **pursue** our Purpose!*

There is nothing inherently *wrong* with breathing, just as there is nothing inherently *wrong* with being the highest-paid person in your company or making a substantial company profit. You have to breathe to live. You have to earn money to provide shelter and put food on the table. Your company has to turn a profit in order to continue doing what it does. *But breathing, earning a salary, and turning a profit are all activities that make purposeful living possible. They are not Purposes in and of themselves.*

And I will tell you something else: the excellence of the actions you take that allow you to create value for other people…and thereby *become* the highest-paid person in your company…will be *sustainable* over time only if you stop making excuses, get clear on your own Purpose, and take consistent action on it. And it is the same for companies: build your company around the goal of making the numbers look good every ninety days, and you will find that you are taking a short-term approach that is simply not sustainable and will not deliver your strongest financial results over the long term. Build your company around a clear *Purpose* that drives everything that happens in your organization, and you will set yourself apart from all your competitors, create a culture that moves past excuses, and deliver much better results over the long term.

ACCOUNTABILITY TAKEAWAYS: CHAPTER 7

All of us have numerous excuses for not releasing ourselves to our Purpose, many of them rooted in our early childhood. Among these is our big excuse—the one we buy into most often.

We convince ourselves that excuses are not only valid in the moment, but *real*.

We must listen when our Accountability Partners point out that we are letting an excuse stand in the way of us releasing ourselves to our Purpose.

Many of our excuses are rooted in a faulty or limited sense of our Purpose in life.

Our Purpose is not the same as the activities we do to support our Purpose. Those are called goals, and they can be distractions from our true Purpose.

If we build our company around a clear *Purpose* that drives everything that happens in our organization, we will set ourselves apart from all competitors, create a culture that moves past excuses, and deliver much better results over the long term.

CHAPTER 8

THE CURE
FOR BURNOUT

DO YOU SOMETIMES FEEL stressed out, off track, spread too thin, or simply lost in a vast maze of urgent priorities? Do you ever wonder where you are headed, personally or professionally...and then find yourself wondering whether maybe, just maybe, you are drifting toward a destination you never chose, a destination called "burnout"?

Guess what? Those feelings and wonderings are all *symptoms*. The big question is: What are they symptoms *of*?

You might be tempted to say that they are symptoms of inadequate or poorly implemented "stress management" techniques. But I have a different answer to suggest: those feelings and wonderings are symptoms of a lack of clarity about your own *unique, deeply personal sense of Purpose*.

You know by now that each of us has our own big *Why*—our own unique Purpose. The challenge is that at any given moment, we may not have recognized that Purpose. We may not have released ourselves to it. We may have lost sight of it momentarily...or we may even have bought into an excuse that prevents us from making decisions that align with that Purpose. Yet as long as we are above ground and breathing, that unique Purpose is always there, waiting for us to internalize it and take action on it.

This Purpose can drive everything we do as we move through our day and our life. We can seek to live it and act in alignment with it. When we are On Purpose, our priorities become clear. Our work becomes play. Our path becomes joyous, not stressful, because we know who we really are and we are in tune with what we really need to do *right now*. This is not to say that we will not get tired (or even exhausted) in the face of any given challenge. But if our relational and tactical commitments align with our unique Purpose, we will tap into a limitless source of energy and achieve what we need to achieve in the moment.

OUR COMMITMENTS MUST ALIGN WITH OUR PURPOSE

 A truly accountable person makes relational and tactical commitments that align with their unique Purpose.

Here, then, is the antidote to "burnout": being fully present in the moment and identifying and acting on our unique Purpose with commitments that align with that Purpose. This is good news.

And here is even better news: Each of us has the opportunity to articulate that Purpose in such a way that it inspires us *constantly* and moves us into a realm of joyous engagement, a realm where it is easy and natural to move instantly beyond the experience of "stress."

But there is a catch. Our Purpose must be focused on *people,* and it must be unique to us. It cannot be based on superficial things, and it cannot be the result of peer pressure. When I ask people suffering from "stress" and "burnout" to tell me their unique Purpose, their reason for being here on this earth, I sometimes hear answers like this:

☞ To make a million dollars.

☞ To drive a Ferrari.

☞ To become a famous (whatever).

Notice that these kinds of answers are focused on *money*, *possessions*, and *status*, respectively. That is an instant tipoff to me that the individual in question has let society set his or her individual Purpose. That is a ticket to the destination called "burnout."

Beating burnout is really a matter of knowing ourselves, being present in our own thought lives, releasing ourselves to our true Purpose, and then taking the actions and the decisions we were born to take.

It helps to have a single, powerful statement that instantly reminds us of who we really are and, by extension, what we need to be doing *right now*. Again, just for reference, my Purpose is:

To help people discover their potential and be the best they can possibly be.

This proclamation is like a compass. It always points in the same direction. It always tells me where I need to go.

Once we get clear on our unique Purpose, once we express it in words, we have a compass, a self-correcting mechanism we can take advantage of in a heartbeat. I call this concise expression of Purpose a *Statement of Purpose*.

Using our Statement of Purpose, we can move past excuses like "I am just too tired" or "I do not have the experience I need" or "I do not get the support I deserve"—or any other excuse. Hanging on to those excuses creates "stress" and "burnout." Excuses take us Off Purpose.

DECISIONS SHOULD NOT STRESS YOU OUT

 At any given moment, we are either On Purpose or Off Purpose. When we are Off Purpose, we feel this thing called "stress," and we experience our decisions as difficult. When we are On Purpose, though, decisions are easy. We have a clear sense of direction that makes "stress" vanish into insignificance and "burnout" irrelevant.

When we are On Purpose—even when what we are doing takes effort or involves making a sacrifice of some kind—we can experience a special kind of joy, a sense of accomplishment, a flow that we can incorporate into our lives with astonishing ease. Good things seem to happen when we are in that flow. We may not even realize that we are "working" or "solving problems." We are just releasing ourselves *from* our excuses and *to* our unique Purpose. We are fulfilling the potential of our very best self, the person we were born to become.

Many of the people I work with who say they are suffering from "burnout" are actually suffering from something very different: a lack of clarity about their own unique Purpose! All too often, they have let someone else set their Purpose for them. And here is how you can tell when you have allowed another person, or society at large, to set your Purpose for you: *your stated Purpose is all about things and not about people.*

Understand: There is nothing inherently *wrong* with possessions, money, and status. But if those things are what are motivating your actions and guiding your decisions, you have bought into an aspiration that does not support you. You are Off Purpose. Things can be a goal… but things can never be a Purpose.

PURPOSE AND SERVICE

 A truly accountable person has a unique sense of Purpose that is rooted in *service* to others.

A truly accountable person makes relational and tactical commitments that align with their unique Purpose.

That unique Purpose is what motivates them, sets their priorities, and guides them through their day!

Society often puts things in front of us that we *mistake* for our Purpose, things like popularity or sensory gratification or cash or recognition. *These are things, not people.* So: Are you serving things... or people? If you are focusing all your effort and attention on things and not on people, you have not yet released yourself to your true Purpose—and you are headed, sooner or later, for trouble!

We have to discover for ourselves, concretely, what our own unique Purpose is—and then we have to stay On Purpose. If we do not do that, we are subject to the manipulations of others and of society at large. If we do not take the time to identify and act on our own Purpose, we may find ourselves acting in support of someone else's agenda—an agenda that may not align with who we really are.

JUST SAY "YET"

Many people I talk to tell me that they do not know what their Purpose is. This is true enough, if we add the word *yet*. So if that is where you are, say: "I do not know what my Purpose is...*yet*." At a deep level, your Purpose is there. You just have not discovered it. You do not have enough clarity to be able to express and act on that Purpose consistently. But that is about to change.

Make no mistake: Identifying our Purpose takes effort. If we have not yet done the self-examination necessary to identify and begin refining our own Purpose, that is no crime. We need to understand, though, that our Purpose is always waiting for us, always lighting the way for us, whether we realize it or not. The minute we say, "I do not have a Purpose," we have done ourselves and the whole human family a disservice. *We do have a Purpose. Our Purpose is our birthright as human beings. We just need to get better at identifying and acting on it.* The actions we need to take to act on our Purpose may not be immediately clear to us, but the more time we spend On Purpose, the clearer the steps will become to us as we go forward.

The fact that we have not yet identified our Purpose does not mean we do not have a Purpose. All it means is that it is time to make finding our Purpose and getting more clarity about it a priority in our life. This priority is one we overlook at our own peril. If we do not take the time to identify our Purpose, we create a void in our own life, and that void will eventually catch up with us. The longer we put it off, the harder the journey to discovering our Purpose will be later on.

THE JOY TEST

Let me share with you one classic scenario where a lack of clarity about Purpose creates a steadily deepening problem and, eventually, a crisis.

Assume, for example, that your father and your grandfather were both attorneys, and assume, too, that they were each financially successful within that profession. Finally, assume that there is pressure within the family for you to follow in your father's and grandfather's footsteps and pursue a career in law. You are ambivalent about this. You do not feel drawn toward law as a calling in life. But there comes a point where you decide to do what your family wants you to do instead of figuring out what *you* want to do. And one of the reasons you make this decision is a belief that you can make a lot of money as an attorney.

So that is what you do. You become an attorney. You make a lot of money. You never stop to ask yourself, "Does this bring me joy?"

Years pass. Decades pass. You pursue a career that does not make you happy, a career that gives you money but does not give you joy. You fail the joy test.

ASK YOURSELF: WHERE IS THE JOY?

Where there is no joy,
there is no Purpose.

Joy is a function of fulfillment, and fulfillment is a sign of Purpose. If your bank account looks good but your fulfillment account, your joy account, looks bleak, you have a problem. You are pursuing goals at the expense of Purpose—*things* rather than *service*. But let's say you choose to ignore that your joy account is continually looking bleaker. Let's say you keep marching in lockstep along the path that someone else has chosen for you, and you justify that poor decision by doubling down on your decision to make your life all about making a lot of money as an attorney. Mind you, there are plenty of ways to be an attorney who acts On Purpose and who serves people in the process. For instance, you might have the Purpose of protecting people who need protection, or of helping families, or of being a voice for people who do not have a voice in the legal system, or of making the tax system as equitable as possible for your clients, or of supporting a justice system that upholds the principle that people are innocent until proven guilty. There are any number of ways to make a lot of money fulfilling Purposes like the ones I have mentioned. But there is no way to be an attorney who acts On Purpose *solely to generate revenue.*

Again: Money is a thing. There is nothing inherently wrong with earning a lot of money. We need money to live, and making money when you are aligned with your Purpose means you can make your own life and the lives of others better. But money is a means to an end—not an end in and of itself. If you make the acquisition of money your Purpose in life, you are setting yourself up for a major fall.

At some point—perhaps in your forties, or your fifties, or your sixties—you will experience a crisis. Maybe it will happen when you consider retiring. Maybe it will happen before that, when you realize that you do not really enjoy being an attorney and can no longer justify devoting your life to a profession that does not inspire you to be and do your best. The lack of joy and fulfillment in your life will create a gap that you cannot get around by buying new cars, or new clothes, or new toys. You will feel this gap more deeply with every passing day. It is the gap that is always caused by ignoring our true Purpose in life, our true calling, our deepest desire to serve. Our Purpose is what connects us to others. If we ignore it, if we make no effort to identify and pursue it, if we pretend that we have no need for a connection with others that ties into something we were born to pursue, then we will eventually find ourselves in a dark hole of our own making. And that hole can be very, very difficult to climb out of.

Rest assured that you can do well financially *and* stay On Purpose. You can work at a job that pays little or nothing and stay On Purpose.

You can have *no* job and stay on Purpose. But you cannot be joyless if you are staying On Purpose.

You may not have *discovered* your Purpose yet. That is fine, but know that you have a Purpose and that it is your job, and no one else's, to discover it. You may well find that it makes sense to keep on being an attorney but that your best path lies in becoming a very different *kind* of attorney: one with a Purpose.

YOUR JOB

 It is your job, and no one else's, to identify your Purpose and create a sense of personal fulfillment through service.

If you are not consistently experiencing joy in your life, it is highly unlikely that you have discovered and taken action on your Purpose, regardless of the amount of money you make. If there is a fulfillment gap in your life, do yourself a favor and close that gap—by gaining clarity on your Purpose and living it! The next chapters will show you how.

ACCOUNTABILITY TAKEAWAYS: CHAPTER 8

If your stated Purpose is all about things and not about people, it is not your true Purpose.

A truly accountable person has a unique sense of Purpose that is rooted in service to others.

A truly accountable person makes tactical and relational commitments that align with that unique Purpose.

If you are not consistently experiencing joy in your life, it is highly unlikely that you have discovered and taken action on your Purpose, regardless of the amount of money you make.

It is your job, and no one else's, to identify your Purpose and create a sense of personal fulfillment through service.

CHAPTER 9

DOES PURPOSE CHANGE OVER TIME?

DOES OUR PURPOSE change over time? Can we experience something of great magnitude and move on to a new Purpose in our life? Questions like these come up often. I believe they are worth considering closely, because the answer is a powerful one: we are continually rediscovering and refining our Purpose. That is part of our job as human beings.

If we release ourselves to our Purpose, if we learn to notice our excuses and move past them, then our Purpose will become clearer and clearer to us as time passes and as our circumstances change. And something else will happen: we will get better and better at putting our Purpose into words. But fundamentally, it is always the same Purpose, the same driving force that we recognize in our heart as uniquely ours. Our task is to get better at noticing its true dimensions.

OUR PURPOSE BECOMES CLEARER OVER TIME

 If we release ourselves to our Purpose, if we learn to notice our excuses and move past them, then our Purpose will become clearer and clearer to us as time passes and our life circumstances change.

Putting our Purpose into words is a vitally important step, because it inspires us to take more and deeper action on our big *Why*. Taking that action eventually gives us new distinctions and new insights that help us find more powerful, more precise words that do an even better job of inspiring us to take action. So this is an ongoing cycle.

As that cycle plays out, our Purpose does not really "change"— we just get better at recognizing and expressing it. We are continually discovering and rediscovering our Purpose, releasing ourselves to it, and expressing it ever more clearly. We must experience for ourselves, over and over again, exactly what our big *Why* is. That *Why* must become clearer and clearer to us as we journey through life.

I realize what I am saying here may sound a little abstract. My accountability partner Mike Domritz's experience with this will help clarify the kind of uniquely personal progression I am talking about.

MIKE'S STORY

"For me, Purpose is all about finding the fire. What is the fire in your heart, the motivating force that brings real energy and direction to your life, no matter what the situation is? It takes most of us a while to find that force and describe it in a way that makes it easy not only to talk about it with others but also to tap into it at any time. Finding the fire was—and is—a journey. For me, that journey has had a number of pivotal moments.

"The first defining moment on that journey came when I was in college, when I got a phone call from my Mom—the worst phone call of my life. She gave me the devastating news that my sister Cheri had been raped. As you can imagine, the weeks and months that followed were a traumatic period for everyone in our family. Life really wasn't the same for any of us after that. I felt a deep rage at the horror of what had happened to Cheri. Little did I realize how much that phone call would define my life's Purpose.

"Six months after that, I heard a professional speaker give a powerful talk on preventing sexual assault. I was transfixed. I felt a deep and compelling sense of certainty—that fire in my heart I mentioned earlier. I thought to myself, 'I want to do that. I want to use my voice to make a difference.' I went up to the speaker after the program and said, 'I want to do what you do. Will you help me learn how to do that?' He said yes and gave me his contact information. He told me to reach out to him.

"That's exactly what I did. I set up a face-to-face meeting with him. When I showed up, he was surprised. 'Lots of people tell me they want to do what I do,' he said, 'but hardly anyone actually shows up to learn how.' We began to talk.

"I wanted to know everything: all the research, all the strategies, all the advice he could possibly give me about getting started as a speaker on this subject. Fortunately, he gave me everything I asked for and then some.

"Soon after, I went to my local high school and asked a teacher I had known for years, Mrs. Farrell, 'Can I give this talk to the students in your class?' She said, 'Sure.' So I gave the speech for the first time, and the response was very positive. Mrs. Farrell told me, 'Mike, this is what you ought to be doing!'

"I felt like I was where I belonged. The one comment by Mrs. Farrell moved me. With her words in mind, I was committed to making a difference—to stopping sexual assault from happening to others. This speech was my medium for doing so. I felt like I was on fire, in a good way—like there was a fire right in the center of my heart. The whole experience had a major impact on me, as did the feedback I got from other people as I started to share the speech with a larger audience.

"I set about the task of using my voice to make a difference in the world about something that really mattered to me…at which point something happened to me. I've learned since that what happened to me happens to just about everyone when they're exploring their Purpose and trying to figure out exactly what its dimensions are. I hit an obstacle.

"At the time, this challenge seemed insurmountable. The obstacle was that I wanted to devote my life to doing this work and thus I had to find a way to get paid to speak in order to survive. To get people to pay me to deliver a program on sexual assault, I was going to have to overcome one specific preconception. It was this one: *you are too young to speak authoritatively on this important topic.*

"A word or two of explanation is in order here. I looked a lot younger than I actually was at the time. When I was 24, I looked like I was about 16. While looking young may seem like a gift, my youthful appearance was a major problem. Educators and administrators struggled with trusting such a young-looking speaker on such a sensitive topic. As if that weren't enough, I also found out that virtually no schools at that time were comfortable bringing in anyone—not even professionals with doctorates—to talk about the topic as a paid speaker. *When I accepted this as the reality of the situation that faced me, I was buying into an excuse.*

"For almost a decade, I focused on other opportunities. I coached high school swimming. I built a mobile DJ entertainment company. And I still spoke once in a while.

"Then, when I was 32, I went to a National Speakers Association event. Someone I respected a lot, Patty Hendrickson, asked me to deliver my program on sexual assault prevention to the kids of the professional speakers who were attending the national conference. I agreed to do that, and the response was overwhelming. The leaders and parents (all professional speakers) who saw me deliver the program that day said things like, 'Wow—you should be focusing on this full time!' That kind of feedback had an impact on me. I felt that fire in my heart again.

"Two weeks later, I sold the mobile DJ entertainment company, and I made a personal commitment to build my speaking business around this one program. I released myself from all the excuses. Society was in a different place, so I focused on making a difference with my voice and specifically on making a difference *on this one topic:* stopping sexual assault.

"It was not easy. I nearly went bankrupt. I did go into massive debt. After living and breathing the task of growing my speaking business for a solid year, the program finally started to take off. The word was getting out about my program, and the demand for it grew dramatically.

"Once my speaking career started to take off, I stayed *on message.* As I launched the program and as I delivered it around the country, here is what that message was: *Ask First. Intervene. Support Survivors.* That all made sense. My Purpose was to keep what happened to my sister from happening to others! I was loving the work and the people I got to work with.

"The journey was in a new phase—a busy one. I was on the road a lot, flying from place to place to share my Purpose—working to stop sexual assault. For a long time, I *thought* that was what my life was all about.

"I started designing training for other people to deliver that shared the same skills I was talking about on stages around the world. The number of people we were getting the message out to grew yet again. When we conducted these training programs for the US Military and crisis center professionals, the feedback was once again overwhelmingly positive. People told me they wanted more of this kind of training. Around the same time, I was also being asked to share with military leaders any ideas I had about how they could help transform their organizational culture into a healthier, more positive version of the culture they had.

"My journey was taking me down new roads. I had to address a new question: *How do all these different programs fit into my Purpose? Is my Purpose broader than it was when I got started? Or am I maybe just noticing how big it really is?*

"While I was wrestling with these questions, something extraordinary happened. I attended a personal development program one weekend that challenged me to come up with a single sentence—a sentence that would drive me powerfully to take action once I made the firm decision to put that sentence right at the center of my life. In short, this assignment challenged me to define my Purpose in a way that would INSPIRE others to take action—people who were not part of the development program and who had never heard of me or my company.

"In essence, I was forced to ask myself: *What is my fire that will ignite the flame for others?*

"As a speaker and author I had always been focused on teaching 'how to' skills. I was all about positive outcomes, but I noticed that weekend that my original Purpose of 'Stop Sexual Assault' started with a word most people consider a negative: 'Stop.'

"I thought to myself, 'Wait a second. I'm known for being positive and my purpose starts with a negative word.' This was a moment of truth. I realized I had to address this essential question: *Was my stated Purpose incongruent with who I really was? Was it bigger than I had acknowledged up to that point?* If it was, I knew I needed to update it.

"I started thinking about this in greater depth than I ever had before. I realized that whenever people would ask what I do, whether at a social gathering or when sitting next to me on a plane, and I would answer by saying that I was committed to stopping sexual assault, the response was often somber and subdued. There was always a dramatic pause, and eventually the person would say something like, 'That's very special, the work you are doing. We need more like you.'

"I had to admit to myself that what these responses lacked was a sense of enthusiasm—of wanting to learn more, of wanting to join the same journey I was on. In fact, when I began the conversation by talking about how I wanted to 'stop sexual assault,' people found ways to change the subject. They quickly found ways to move the conversation into a different, more positive area. They'd ask me questions such as how many countries I'd spoken in or what media outlets I'd been interviewed by. They almost never wanted to discuss the work itself.

"This realization led me to another series of questions: *What if the way I defined and expressed my Purpose truly aligned, not just with the positive outcome I was after, but also with my personal energy of positivity? What if a new definition of my Purpose could lead to the outcome of reducing sexual assault while at the same time increasing healthy relationships? What if I took a more positive focus?*

"I wrote down, and later spoke, this sentence: *I want to help build a world of mutually amazing consensual sex!*

"When I read that sentence out loud, I found my heart was on fire again. This was a new flame—burning brighter and higher than ever before. This was absolutely positive. If everyone, and I do mean everyone, who was sexually active pursued *only* mutually amazing consensual sex, then sexual assault would become a thing of the past, which was of course what I wanted. I knew I was onto something transformative.

"The other participants in the program that weekend were genuinely excited by the Purpose I shared. One of them said, 'I want more of that!' This new definition of my Purpose was where I belonged. I knew it.

"In programs where it was age appropriate, I started teaching about 'Mutually Amazing Consensual Sex.' The response was incredible.

Educators and military leaders were asking, "This approach is such a game changer. Why didn't we learn this sooner?"

"So—story over, right? I finally defined my Purpose, didn't I? Hold on.

"I had many friends who had built amazing reputations and businesses speaking to corporations and associations. These friends started asking me, 'Mike, why are you not speaking to companies? Your style and approach would work perfectly with those audiences.'

"My immediate reaction was, 'Companies are not going to hire a speaker to teach how to build a world of mutually amazing consensual sex.' I had a reason—an excuse—for why I wasn't right for that market. That work (I thought) didn't fit into my Purpose.

"But my friends didn't give up on me. They kept asking me these questions. One of them asked me, 'What if you could teach the exact same skill sets as you do in your other work—except customize it for businesses and associations?' A light bulb went off in my mind. Actually, it was more like an explosion. I asked myself: *What if my Purpose was to help build Mutually Amazing Relationships?*

"My journey seemed to be experiencing another one of those life-altering moments. I thought, *Wait a moment. What if that really IS my Purpose? How would 'Mutually Amazing Relationships' fit into all of my work?*

"Well, parents and individuals are certainly in relationships: building mutually amazing relationships is the ultimate way to love yourself and another. That part fit.

"What about middle schools, high schools, universities, and the US military? They fit, too. If students and our military members had mutually amazing relationships as their standard, everyone's boundaries would be honored and respected. People would not pressure others into sexual activity and/or experimentation. Not only that—mutually amazing relationships would mean we looked out for each other and intervened in dangerous situations. Mutually amazing relationships would also mean we proactively create safe spaces for survivors.

"How about businesses and associations? Well, if everyone in an organization was focused on building mutually amazing relationships in the workplace, each person would be respected and equally valued. Each person would feel safe sharing their concerns and/or ideas. People would treat each other with care. Liabilities and risks in companies would be greatly reduced…and retention and productivity would soar.

"I had what can best be described as an OMG moment! This new personal Purpose—building Mutually Amazing Relationships—was not just on fire; it was ablaze! And it aligned with everything I was doing and wanted to do. This newly refined Purpose crushed every possible roadblock and obstacle. A clear path was awaiting me.

"Our company's Mission—and mine—is building mutually amazing relationships at home, at school, in the workplace, and everywhere else. That is my Purpose in action. A side note: Respect is the key to building a mutually amazing relationship.

"Today, I am grateful to have a deeper clarity on my Purpose than ever before: in my heart and my soul, the fire is all about teaching the daily skills and strategies for building mutually amazing relationships—founded in a culture of respect.

"I believe we all need to ask ourselves, from time to time, *What is my fire?*—and then listen to the answer that comes back. I also believe we must be willing to ask ourselves, 'Is my stated Purpose limiting me or my ability to make a bigger impact? Does my Purpose align with my energy and my strengths?' As time goes on, as we gain more insights about ourselves and the world in which we live, we can become clearer and clearer about our Purpose. Our Purpose does not change, in my opinion, so much as *we* change in our ability to perceive it, act on it, and define it.

"Looking back at the very beginning of my journey, I can now see how my current Purpose was always present. I simply needed more experiences and wisdom to better define it. What about 10 years from now? Ask me then. I can't wait to find out."

THE TWO MORALS OF MIKE'S STORY

I hope you can see why Mike is one of my Accountability Partners. He has been extremely important in my life, and I think he would say that I have made a difference in his. Our Accountability Partnership has been a very significant relationship for both of us.

Here are the two big takeaways I get from Mike's inspiring story. First, it is a huge mistake not to search for, and refine, your life's Purpose. The longer you wait to begin this search, the more you will regret having put it off.

Second, it is just as huge a mistake to assume that once you express your Purpose in words, you have completed the journey. If your life journey is not over, the journey to express and fulfill your Purpose is not over. Your Purpose will become clearer to you over time, and it may require different words, but precisely the same driving force will be animating your life.

In the next chapter, I will share five critical questions you can use to identify and refine your unique Purpose.

ACCOUNTABILITY TAKEAWAYS: CHAPTER 9

We are continually rediscovering and refining our Purpose, releasing ourselves to it, and learning to express it ever more clearly.

It is a huge mistake not to search for, and refine, your life's Purpose. The longer you wait to begin this search, the more you will regret having put it off.

It is just as huge a mistake to assume that once you express your Purpose in words, you have completed the journey.

If your life journey is not over, the journey to express and fulfill your Purpose is not over.

CHAPTER 10

FIVE POWERFUL QUESTIONS
ABOUT PURPOSE

SOMETHING EXTRAORDINARY happens when you are fully living your Purpose: a powerful feeling of not only being connected in a deeper way to the human family, but also living in unity with a higher power, a higher calling. There is a feeling of being in complete alignment with something far larger than ourselves.

The poet Jane Hirshfield wrote: **"We feel like separate water droplets—but we are also ocean."** Those powerful words sum up, for me, exactly what it feels like when I am On Purpose: the feeling of being the ocean, not just a single drop of water. I suspect her words remind you, too, of the times when you felt absolutely certain that you were doing the right thing with your life.

With the memory of that important feeling in mind, it is time to start clarifying your Purpose and releasing yourself to it fully. This requires a certain amount of self-assessment. That self-assessment begins now, with the five critical questions covered in this chapter.

My strong recommendation is that you start out by answering all of these questions in writing.

Question One:
Whom Do You Serve?

Our Purpose connects us to our best personal understanding of how we can serve others. Our Purpose will always connect us to some service that we are providing to other people. Sometimes, we make the mistake of believing that the simple fact that we are good at something makes that thing our Purpose. Wrong. Whatever it is we do well *must connect to some kind of service.* If you believe you have found your Purpose but it does not connect to another person, keep looking!

Take at least five minutes to identify, in writing, one or more specific people you have served when you were feeling true joy.

This service should not feel like a burden. It should feel like who you really are. You might say you felt the most joy when you were serving children who needed your help. You might say you felt the most joy when you were serving your company's customers. You might say you felt the most joy when you were taking care of your family. It is entirely dependent on your own experience...but *you have to serve somebody.* Find out who that was and what the service you provided was. Most important, find out for yourself *why* you felt joy in doing what you did.

Question Two:
What Is Most Important to You?

Your personal Declaration of Purpose must connect to something that truly matters to you as an individual. So take some time to consider *what is more important to you than anything else?*

I realize that this question can be a little intimidating at first, so I have broken it down into a series of sub-questions. Write at least one sentence in response to each of the following prompts, and you will find that you have edged closer to an answer to the larger question of what is truly important to you.

- What is important to you on a daily basis? What was most important to you yesterday, for instance? Why was that important?

- What specific personal goals are most important to you?

- Why are they important now?

- What have you done recently that supports what is important to you? For instance, how does what you did yesterday connect to what is most important to you? Be specific.

- If you own a business: How does your business connect to what you just identified as important?

- Regardless of whether you own a business: Are you looking to get or to give? How do you know? What actions support your answer? WHAT are you looking to give, and to whom?

Spend between ten and fifteen minutes creating *written* answers to the questions above. Understand that these questions are meant to begin the conversation—not end it. By asking yourself these and other tough questions and opening yourself up to new possibilities by noticing where the answers lead you, you are laying the groundwork for identifying *that which is important to you in all situations.* Note that if you own a business, it will be important for you to make sure that the answers you give for your business must not conflict with the answers you give as an individual. If you say that supporting honesty and integrity is important to you on a daily basis as an individual, your business must not be based on deception.

Question Three:
What Would a Single Sentence That Expresses That Sound Like?

This is where you make it happen. Look carefully at all that you have written down, and take all the time you need to distill your most powerful responses into a single sentence. Expect to refine your words as you seek clarity and connection with your Purpose.

This question is a game changer. Give yourself the time you need to come up with a powerful sentence that speaks the truth from your heart and to your heart. This is your Declaration of Purpose.

A good friend of mine, a writer, used this formula to create the following Declaration of Purpose:

> **To express devotion to my Creator by loving people and supporting them.**

That is what works for him. That is his "dolly zoom." He re-enters and re-releases himself to his Purpose every time he reads those words. He uses his Statement of Purpose to spot and get past his favorite excuse: "It's good enough." This Purpose expresses itself not just in interactions where he feels familiar or comfortable interacting with someone he knows, but in interactions with total strangers.

When you find the Purpose that launches your "dolly zoom," you will know it. You will feel like you know who you are and exactly what you need to do next. By putting this one sentence into writing, you are really answering the powerful question *Who am I?* Once you understand that, you will understand your own big *Why*. Just as businesses must understand *why* they are in business in the first place before they focus on *what* they are doing and *how* they are going to go about doing it, you must delve into the *why* before you start trying to figure out the *what* and the *how*.

Think about what feels good and right for you. Think about what brings you joy. Then, based on what you have uncovered about yourself, spend at least fifteen minutes creating a draft of your one-sentence Declaration of Purpose. Do this before you move on to the next question.

Remember: This is an ongoing process. Years from now, you may still be looking at your Declaration of Purpose and asking yourself, *Have I captured it?* That is the nature of this enterprise. You will become clearer and clearer in your expression of your Purpose the more time you spend On Purpose. But do not let that fact keep you from getting as clear as you can possibly be *right now* about the language that inspires you most *right now*. Once you have found that language, reward yourself! Find some way to celebrate!

Question Four:
Have You Released Yourself to Your Purpose?

Releasing yourself to your Purpose means consciously accepting it as the guiding force of your life. It also means releasing yourself *from* all excuses.

You will know when this happens because you will feel a deep sense of calm. You will no longer feel that you are being pulled in multiple directions. You will know your direction in life, whether you are having a good day or a bad day, whether things are lining up the way you expected or they are not. Decisions will become much easier for you. You know immediately if you are acting in the service of your Purpose.

That sense of calm is where you are meant to be headed. It is the starting point of any discussion about your Mission, your Values, or your commitments, which means it is the starting point of any discussion about accountability. That is why it is so important that you spend the time necessary to figure this out and put it into words that clarify and refine your Purpose. You cannot participate in an Accountability Circle without that understanding and that language.

Notice that what we are talking about here is not tactical. Even though this is the foundation of everything that follows here, it is not the first step of some simple seven-step program. It is every step. It is basic self-awareness, brought to a critical level of priority, by means of understanding and language. Not everyone has figured out why they are here on earth well enough to put it into words, but some people have. *My challenge to you now is to become the kind of person who knows their Purpose and is comfortable talking about it.*

Question Five:
What Are Your Obstacles?

Even after we release ourselves to our Purpose, even after we feel ourselves strongly motivated to take action on it, we are going to hit obstacles. Some examples of obstacles are...

Lack of experience. Most of us are not used to focusing on our Purpose. It takes practice. The very first time you drove a car, you were not ready to take the vehicle out on the highway at full speed. You needed some practice, some time behind the wheel, before highway driving became second nature to you. Give yourself that time behind the wheel, and be gentle with yourself as you learn and master the power of focusing on your Statement of Purpose. Review it regularly. Then, each time you create a "dolly zoom moment" for yourself, go back to the Three Big Questions. Just as a reminder, they are:

 What do I believe?

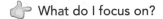 What do I focus on?

 What do I commit to?

Holding yourself to an impossibly high standard. Another obstacle is the common mistake of holding ourselves to an impossible standard. Noticing when we are On Purpose and when we are Off Purpose is part of life. It is not an excuse to beat ourselves up when we find that we are Off Purpose. No one is perfect.

This is not about being perfect. It is about being better. Ask yourself: "When I am Off Purpose—meaning, when I notice that I am making decisions that are not in alignment with my Purpose—how will I course correct compassionately, without beating myself up?" Take a few minutes to design some strategies.

For instance, sometimes I fall into the trap of being judgmental with other people. I may see someone who is doing something more slowly than I would do it, or who is less attentive than I want them to be, or who is late sending me something, and I may think to myself, "That is a lazy person." It upsets me when I do this, because I know that is not who I want to be. I may know something about the behavior I am seeing, but I really do not know anything about what the person is going through or who that person is. So I have to be honest with myself and recognize when something is not right. I have to admit that when I am being judgmental, I am not being the best I can be, and I have to acknowledge that I cannot help others be the best they can be if I am not being the best I can be.

But there is something else I have to take into account. Whenever I notice this judgmental attitude taking over my perception of someone, does it really make sense for me to kick myself around the block for ten or twenty minutes, or even one minute? Does it really make sense for me to feel guilty about what a terrible choice I made to judge that other person? No. That would be a waste of time and energy. Once you acknowledge that you are Off Purpose and that you may be acting in a way you do not want to be, focus on getting back On Purpose. This is what your Statement of Purpose is for! Return to it often. Remember, you can always use it to generate a "dolly zoom moment."

The big excuse. A third obstacle, and one that I believe everyone must find a way to deal with, is our big excuse—the excuse we use most often, or perhaps even use automatically, to justify going Off Purpose. Each of us should know what that excuse is for us. If you haven't already done so, it is worth taking the time to work this out right now. Think about the examples I have shared with you. Mike shared that his excuse was that he was too young and inexperienced. For Chief Brody in *Jaws*, the big excuse was "There is nothing I can do." My excuse is "I cannot show my weaknesses." A good friend of mine has the big excuse of "I am too busy for this."

What is your big excuse? Take at least five minutes to write down the go-to story you tell yourself and try to sell to others to justify going Off Purpose. Once you know what your big excuse is, you can get better at noticing when you are hiding behind it! Eventually, you will want to share what you have learned with your Accountability Partners.

Again, releasing yourself to your Purpose means releasing yourself FROM all excuses!

It is not easy to identify and talk about your excuses. It is not easy to confront them and face your own justifications, some of which may have been built up over a period of years or even decades. And it is certainly not easy to step away from them once you have identified them. A big part of what we are acknowledging in this early part of the accountability process is the reality that we are going to need help with all of that from our Accountability Partners. They can help us awaken ourselves to what is really going on when we hide behind our big excuse.

We need to prepare ourselves internally for the reality that some tough questions are inevitably going to come our way, and we need to be open to them. Within the Accountability Circle, we need to allow that to happen, and we need to show a vulnerability and a willingness to listen that we may have never shown before in our lives. We need to be coachable.

You want the kind of relationship where the other person can call a time-out, look you in the eye, and say, "Hey, do you remember when you told me your big excuse was 'It's good enough'? I think that may be happening right here. You might need to stop and look at that."

It is okay for this relationship to be a bit adversarial—in a healthy, constructive, and respectful way—from time to time. In fact, it is absolutely essential that it be so. That is how accountability works within the Circle. If we do not acknowledge, to ourselves and to our Accountability Partners, that there are going to be times when we are going to need help seeing that we are hiding behind our big excuse, then we are not working this process.

IS THE CIRCLE IN INTEGRITY?

If an Accountability Partner decides not to mention when he or she notices that you are hiding behind an excuse, the Accountability Circle is out of integrity, and your partner has let you down.

By the same token, if you decide not to say anything when you notice that your partner is hiding behind an excuse, you are letting your partner down.

In an Accountability Circle, there is always a connective tissue between my Purpose and your Purpose, and it lies in compassionately calling each other out on our excuses so that we can stay On Purpose and keep moving forward.[4] When you help me recognize when I am making an excuse that takes me Off Purpose, and I do the same for you, we will each get better at noticing and fulfilling our Purpose. We will spend more of our precious time On Purpose.

HAVE YOU DONE ALL THAT?

An understanding of your unique Purpose and the Purposes of each of your Accountability Partners is the connective tissue that keeps

---

4   If you are starting a company or a nonprofit in partnership with someone, you will also want to make sure that you share your Statement of Purpose with that partner and that you get a clear sense of what his or her Purpose is. I strongly recommend you give that partner a copy of this book and discuss the chapters on Purpose in depth together.

the Accountability Circle alive and functioning. When you know your Purpose, you know you have released yourself to it, and you know what big excuse stands in the way, you will be ready to move on to the next section of the book.

ACCOUNTABILITY TAKEAWAYS: CHAPTER 10

To identify your unique Purpose, ask yourself these questions:

- Whom do I serve?

- What is most important to me?

- What would a single sentence that expresses that sound like?

- Have I released myself to my Purpose?

- What are my obstacles?

CHAPTER 11

ACCOUNTABILITY
AND MISSION

YOUR *MISSION* is your Purpose in action. It is born out of your Purpose.

It is quite common for people (and teams and even entire organizations) to get a little confused about what the Mission is. All too often, people confuse the Mission with the Purpose. That confusion does not exist in a functioning Accountability Circle. Once you get done with this part of the book, it will not exist for you or anyone in your Circle anymore, either.

Just remember:

Your Purpose is the reason you are here, phrased in the form of service that you render to others. Your Purpose is your WHY.

Your Mission, by contrast, is your Purpose IN ACTION. It is something specific that turns that Purpose into a tangible reality for someone else. It is WHAT you do to take action on your Purpose.

You may remember that my Purpose is:

To help people discover their potential and be the best they can possibly be.

That is the north point on my personal Purpose compass. Notice that it is very concise. That one sentence is what I use to determine whether any direction, any idea, any proposed course of action, or any attitude is On Purpose or Off Purpose.

But a compass is not a destination. Neither is my Declaration of Purpose a destination. It is not a place I can actually arrive at in the real world. In order for me to have that kind of practical destination, I need a Mission that matches up with my Purpose. I need to identify that Mission by asking myself, *What actions support and fulfill my Purpose?*

As a general but reliable rule, the personal statement of Mission you create and pursue in your life needs to have more depth and be more detailed than your Declaration of Purpose. I believe the words you use to craft the Mission can and should be built around three action words of your choice. These words should give you and everyone who reads or hears the words a deep and compelling understanding of your Mission. The action words you choose must be unique to you. It is important to notice, though, that those words have to connect to a longer **Mission Narrative.**

We need to dig deep with those three words. We need to clarify everything of consequence that connects to the *actions* we are taking in support of our Purpose. That way we—and others—can see and buy into the *story* of our Purpose in action.

SHARE IT WITH THE WORLD

 Your Mission Narrative must clarify the ACTIONS that support your Purpose. While your Purpose may be uniquely for you, your Mission is meant to be shared with the wider world.

Our Mission Narrative tells us, and anyone else our Mission touches or attracts, exactly what it means to step out and go about achieving the Mission. In fact, that is the whole point of the "three action word" exercise I will be asking you to complete in Chapter 13: to create unmistakable personal clarity about what you are doing in support of your Purpose, the kind of clarity that attracts other people. If you do not have this kind of clarity, not only will *you* not buy into the Mission, but no one else will understand what you are doing or be motivated to buy into it either. It is only when you have deep personal clarity about your own actions that you can attract others to join and support your Mission. You certainly cannot expect your Accountability Partners to support you in pursuing your Mission if you yourself are not crystal clear about what it is.

This is all about *doing.* The kind of personal clarity I am talking about results in immediate *action* that aligns with your Purpose. It is not abstract or theoretical. It is dynamic and totally in sync with your deepest personal reason for being.

This kind of personal clarity has a fascinating effect on people. When you are utterly clear, deep down, about both *why* you are here on earth and *what* you are doing *right now* to support your *why*, something remarkable starts to happen. People get inspired by the double-barreled force of your words and your personal example, as exemplified in your action. They start to notice that your words actually *align* with your actions. They want to know more about both the *why* and the *what*. They look for ways to engage with you so they can figure out for themselves exactly where you are going—and whether they should be doing something to help you get there.

And you know what? Eventually, some of them will join your cause. They will commit themselves with full purpose to your Mission because they have concluded that your Mission matches up with what *they* want to be doing. They will become Allies.

LEADERSHIP IS ABOUT SETTING THE MISSION

There are a lot of different names for the phenomenon that attracts the attention, goodwill, and support of other people to your Mission. Some people call it charisma. Others call it personal magnetism. Others call it star quality. Whatever you choose to call it, what I want you to notice about it is that it is rooted in a total, unconditional connection between your *why* and your *what*. That connection is what causes people to sign on to what you are doing. When the *why* that is driving you is 100 percent clear to you and 100 percent in alignment with your *what*—your decisions and actions—then *people notice*. Your clarity naturally draws others to you. This kind of clarity is an essential prerequisite of true leadership. Note here that I am talking about leadership in your own life, which is your birthright regardless of whether you hold a formal leadership position in an organization.

> ## LEADERSHIP IS OUR BIRTHRIGHT
>
> Leadership is all about establishing the Mission in a way that inspires others to join us. This requires clarity. If we ourselves do not have clarity about the Mission we are undertaking in support of our own Purpose, how can we possibly expect to share that Mission with others? Leadership is our birthright. We must claim it in our own lives.

YOUR MISSION NARRATIVE

The Mission Narrative you will be creating will help you develop the kind of personal clarity about your mission that I am talking about here. You will know you have found the right Mission when you find that writing or talking about it gives you instant calmness. This calmness is addictive, and it is capable of existing side by side with profound excitement about your Mission. This calmness comes from the very center of your being, and it appears only when there is total certainty about both your Purpose and the action steps you are taking to fulfill that Purpose.

By way of example, here is my personal Mission. Notice that it supports and fulfills my Purpose. Notice, too, that I have found three powerful action words to create a Mission Narrative about WHAT I DO that supports my Declaration of Purpose.

This Mission Narrative has resulted in people *all over the world* wanting to be a part of and support my Mission—very often, people I do not even know and have never before spoken to!

MY PERSONAL MISSION

My Mission is to build a more accountable world. I serve my Mission through three specific activities:

TEACH

I am a teacher. I educate people on ways to improve and be their best. I share new insights and ways of looking at issues, challenges, and opportunities. I share different ways of believing and thinking.

INSPIRE

Through the use of events, experiences, and evidence I support the beliefs that I teach. This breathes life into the beliefs and helps people take action. I help people awaken to their true Purpose in life.

SUPPORT

I come alongside and help people take the "first step" in their new adventure. I provide ongoing encouragement, tools, and resources to help people stay on course. Change is difficult. We all face challenges throughout our journey. I stay ready to help others overcome those challenges and achieve the goals they aspire to.

My Mission Narrative makes it clear that my aim of creating an accountable world connects to three specific activities: teaching, inspiring, and supporting. It goes into an appropriate amount of detail about what those words mean to me, for the simple reason that what I mean by "teach" may not be the same as what you mean by the word "teach."[5] If I am going to inspire you to support my Mission, it helps for us both to be clear about exactly what we are talking about. Simply writing down the words *Teach*, *Inspire*, and *Support* does not accomplish that. I must provide context as to what those words mean as I pursue the Mission. In fact, just writing down those words may actually do more harm than good, because when people fill in the blanks on their own, there are inevitably going to be disconnects and communication problems.

The Mission Narrative is extremely important, and it is worth spending some time on, because it clarifies the way you live your Purpose, day in and day out. It is specific. It is action-oriented and goal-oriented. It is the *process* that brings your Purpose into tangible reality, the manifestation of your Purpose as it actually occurs in the world. The Mission Narrative highlights, in no uncertain terms, where your activity is. If what you are actually *doing* every day does not match up with your Mission Narrative, then there is a problem, and you need to fix that problem so that your actions and your Mission Narrative are in complete alignment.

People often ask me, "Does the personal Mission change over time?" What I have discovered is that as time goes on and as relationships change, it may look like the Mission changes. Usually, though, the only thing that has really changed is the relationships that are affected by your Purpose and the language you use to describe the actions you are undertaking as part of the Mission. The direction remains the same. True north is still true north. We just get better at recognizing the best pathways available to us. As we recognize those pathways, we may need to update the language of our Mission Narrative.

---

5   In addition, what I mean by "teach" today may not be the same as what I mean when I use that word at some point down the line. Twenty years from now, my Mission might be to teach a different group of people, such as high school students, and my Narrative could change to reflect that! As time goes by, we can all gain additional insights and make new distinctions about what does and does not support the Mission.

"GET EVERYBODY OUT!" A RETURN TO THE "DOLLY ZOOM MOMENT"

You will recall that earlier in the book, I shared the extraordinary moment in the film *Jaws* when Roy Scheider's character, Chief Brody, is awakened to his Purpose and empowered to move past his excuses: that unforgettable "dolly zoom moment." That kind of awakening is what a clearly defined Purpose is all about. Now it is time to look at the *action* that simultaneously arises from that moment. In other words, it is time to look at Brody's emerging Mission.

Purpose and Mission are really two sides of the same coin. What I mean by that is simply that it is a mistake to think of these two things as existing independently of one another in your life. You can see what I mean if you watch that "dolly zoom moment" scene again. You will see that unforgettable moment where the background recedes into the distance while we in the audience stay fixated on Brody's awestruck face. But that is not all you will see.

Notice what happens right after Brody sees his worst nightmare turned into reality: a shark attack, right in front of him, on a crowded public beach—*his* crowded public beach. *In an instant,* Brody is up and on his feet and rushing to the water. He shouts, "Get everybody out! Get 'em out!"

What I want you to be aware of here is that less than five seconds pass between the moment Brody sees unmistakable evidence of the shark's presence and his decision to take *action* in support of his Purpose: to protect people. When he ran toward the shark attack and started shouting for people to get out of the water, Brody was On Purpose. He was literally a man on a Mission.

LIVING YOUR MISSION MEANS BEING ON PURPOSE

 You are On Purpose when you are making decisions and taking actions that support your Purpose. If you are *not* making decisions and taking actions that support your Purpose, you are Off Purpose. Neither your Purpose nor your Mission are alive in that moment of you being Off Purpose.

Brody's emerging Mission in that terrifying moment on the beach is narrowly focused, but it is clear enough: keep anyone else still in the water—and there are dozens of people out there swimming— from getting attacked by the shark that is, without a doubt, now threatening Amity Island. Notice that his Mission is *inseparable from his Purpose.*

If Chief Brody had been the kind of person who saw a shark attack and instantly ran in the opposite direction without even a thought of protecting others, then he would not really have had the Purpose of protecting people. He might have *said* that was his Purpose, and he might even have found a way to convince himself of it. But if his actions and decisions went in the opposite direction, *that Purpose would not have been alive in him, and it would not have generated a Mission.*

By the same token, if Chief Brody had been the kind of person who saw a shark attack right in front of him and then watched passively, doing nothing to protect those oblivious of the danger nearby, then he would not really have had the Purpose of protecting people. Again, no matter what he might have said, no matter what justifications he might have fed himself, *that Purpose would not have existed in him, and it would not have generated a Mission.*

But that is not the kind of person Chief Brody was. He was the kind of person who, upon seeing a deadly shark attack, ran *straight to the water*, at his own peril, to make absolutely sure that people knew there was a dangerous situation and that they needed to get back on dry land immediately. *Because that Purpose existed powerfully enough in him for him to take action, it generated a Mission.*

THERE IS NO PURPOSE WITHOUT ACTION

 There is no Purpose without action—without a Mission. If someone tells you what their Purpose is but has no idea what actions support that Purpose, *that person is not On Purpose.* Only someone who undertakes actions and makes decisions in support of a clear Purpose can be said to be On Purpose.

Brody's Purpose and the Mission it generates are personally compelling. It is not like he has a choice about whether to run into the ocean. For him, there is no alternative. We do not see him debating with himself about whether it makes sense for him to run into the water. The Purpose is so strong in him that it instantly gives rise to a Mission that defines him as a person because it motivates him to take action in a powerful, impossible-to-ignore way.

That Mission, for Brody, evolves over time. In the aftermath of the beach attack he witnesses, the true dimensions of the Mission before him become obvious to him: he has to kill the shark. But how?

That is a big question, but not a question that paralyzes him. As he ponders that question, the fact that his Mission is 100 percent in alignment with his Purpose is what keeps Chief Brody going. *He* is fully aligned.

Your Mission *must* align with your Purpose if you are to move forward in any meaningful way. If the Mission does not align with the Purpose, you either do not know your Purpose or you are on the wrong Mission. Notice that there are plenty of people in the *Jaws* story who see the same things that Brody does but do not have his Purpose and do not take his action. Some of them even act in direct opposition to him. That is okay. That is what happens when you have a strong Purpose and a strong Mission that aligns with it. You will run into obstacles along the way. The question is, how will you respond?

Last but not least, notice that Brody *elicits and sustains the support of key Allies who assist him in the Mission of killing the shark.* This is the power of a compelling Mission. It attracts people and support. That is vitally important. Why? Because at the moment it becomes clear to Brody that his Mission is to kill the shark that is threatening his community, he literally has no idea how he is going to make that happen. He does not have anything like the skill set necessary to kill a great white shark, he has no resources for doing so, and he has no Allies. But none of this stops him from accepting the Mission. He makes no excuses!

"NOT KNOWING HOW" IS AN EXCUSE

 Failing to take action on the Mission because you do not know how it will be fulfilled, do not have resources or Allies, or do not have experience is an excuse. Do not buy into it. Accept the Mission and take action. Strong Missions that are aligned with your Purpose inspire action that attracts the support of others.

What Brody does have is a strong enough Purpose—*protect people*—to move him forward, *despite the fact that he does not know how he is going to pull off his Mission.* He has a willingness to speak, act, and make decisions in full alignment with his Purpose. To support his Mission of killing the shark, he lobbies the mayor to hire Quint, a professional shark hunter, and he strengthens his relationship with Hooper, an oceanographer who has helped him identify the kind of shark that is threatening the island.

These two people would never have come Brody's way in the absence of Brody's clear action in support of his Purpose and Mission. That is what strong, aligned Missions do. They inspire Action and attract the support of others!

So what happens? Both Quint and Hooper commit to help Brody attain the goal of killing the shark. These three men set out on Quint's boat, the Orca, to hunt down the nameless great white that is threatening the island. They are Brody's Allies.

By the way, there is something extremely important about the *Jaws* story that we need to recognize before we go any further…something about Quint and Hooper. *We have no idea what Purpose is driving Quint. We have no idea what Purpose is driving Hooper.* Neither does Chief Brody. At the time he recruits them as Allies, he does not know what is driving each man at a deep personal level. He has no idea what their Purpose compass is. And that is okay.

We do, however, know a little bit about the Mission that each of those men has undertaken in life before they sign on to Brody's Mission to kill the shark. And since they end up becoming Brody's most important Allies in that effort, their Mission is what you and I need to look at next.

What do we know about Matt Hooper's Mission before he shows up at Amity Island? What actions has he already been taking? What has he been pursuing in life? The answer is: a shark. *This* shark. When we go back to the movie and watch it closely, what we learn is that Hooper is a young, ambitious oceanographer with a theory to prove about the migratory patterns of great white sharks. He has been tracking one specific shark all around the world. He wants to confirm that this is the same shark he has been chasing around the globe, and he wants to kill the shark so he can present his theory—and the shark's carcass—to the Museum of Natural History, thereby establishing himself as a leader in a highly competitive scientific field.

Notice: Brody really wants to kill the shark. Hooper really wants to kill the shark. They have different reasons for taking action, at least at first, but their Missions *align*.

Let me pause here to point out something crucial: Hooper *also* wants to protect people. He never pursues his Mission in a way that endangers the residents of Amity Island. He is deeply upset when people refuse to listen to him about how dangerous this particular shark is. But his Mission started for a whole different reason than Brody's did: Hooper is a scientist, and he wants to prove his theory. Even with a different ultimate goal, however, scruffy Matt Hooper decides that Brody's Mission supports his own Mission, complements his own Mission, *aligns* with his own Mission. So he signs on to Brody's Mission.

What about Quint? Well, what Brody finds out about him during the first third of the movie is limited to two pretty compelling facts. First and foremost, Quint, unlike Brody, knows what he is doing in this line of work. He has a long track record of killing sharks. Big ones. And second, he is good enough at doing this to demand payment for it. So we might at first imagine—just as Brody imagines—that we understand what drives Quint: money.

It turns out, though, that this guy has a fascinating personal history when it comes to great white sharks. Decades before the story began, he was on the USS *Indianapolis*, a (real-life) World War II ship charged with delivering the atomic bomb to a secret location so that it could be used against Japan. On its way back home after delivering the bomb to its secret destination on an obscure Pacific Island, the *Indianapolis* was torpedoed by a Japanese submarine. Those of its crew who survived the initial attack, we learn, found themselves swimming for their lives in shark-infested waters, praying a friendly ship would appear to rescue them. That did not happen for days. Quint was one of the few survivors of the attack. He saw scores of his buddies attacked and killed by great whites. Chief Brody eventually figures out—as we figure out—that even though Quint does want to get paid for his work, he wants something else even more: revenge against any and every great white he can track down. It may have something to do with survivor guilt. It may be revenge. Who knows? Quint is a complicated guy.

Here again, though, we need to observe the key point about *alignment*: Brody really wants to kill the shark. Quint really wants to kill the shark. That part matches up perfectly. In fact, the more we find out about Quint, the more likely it seems that he would be out there prowling the oceans secretly, looking for this monster, whether or not he got paid for doing so. The man is obsessed. What I want to highlight for you, though, is that Quint has a very different driving force for doing what he does than Brody does—or than Hooper does, for that matter. But his Mission aligns with Brody's Mission. So he signs on.

We will return to the *Jaws* example one more time, in Chapter 15, when we discuss Values.

IT TAKES ALL KINDS

 People with wildly different Purposes can and do sign on to the same Mission.

IS YOUR ALLY YOUR ACCOUNTABILITY PARTNER?

Probably not.

Your Mission, by definition, needs Allies. Not every Ally is an Accountability Partner...but anyone with whom you create an Accountability Partner relationship must be an Ally in the sense of buying into and supporting your Mission, just as you must buy into and support theirs.

The question of who we do—and do not—take on as Allies in the Mission is a vitally important one. It is intimately connected to the question of whether the prospective Ally operates under a complementary set of Values to yours. We will be looking closely at Values in Chapters 14–17. For now, just understand that someone whom you attract as an Ally for your Mission will not necessarily be someone you allow into your Accountability Circle.

The person you allow into your Accountability Circle must be a special kind of Ally: someone who knows your Purpose (which not everyone does); someone who knows, aligns with, and supports your Mission (again, not everyone does); and someone who operates under Values that align with yours (not everyone will). Even if someone happens to match up with all three of these criteria, that does not mean that person necessarily belongs in your Accountability Circle. There are all kinds of issues related to personal chemistry and group fit that need to be taken into account.

THE BOTTOM LINE

Your Mission must seamlessly connect to your Purpose, and vice versa. You do not have to know how you are going to complete such a Mission in order to take it on, and in fact it is very likely that you will *not* know how to complete it when you are considering taking it on. *Take it on anyway.* If you create the right Mission and take appropriate action on it, people will come on board and find a way to support it and you, even if their Purpose is different from yours. Without realizing it, you will tap into something deep and important in their lives. Who knows? Your Mission may well position someone else to live their Purpose fully.

Accountability Takeaways: Chapter 11

Your *Mission* is your Purpose in action. It is born out of your Purpose.

Your Mission Narrative must clarify the ACTIONS that support your Purpose. While your Purpose may be uniquely for you, your Mission is meant to be shared with the wider world.

Your Mission Narrative must inspire others to join your Mission.

Failing to take action on the Mission because you do not know how it will be fulfilled, do not have resources or Allies, or do not have experience is an excuse. Do not buy into it. Accept the Mission and take action.

People with wildly different Purposes can and do sign on to the same Mission.

Your Mission may well position someone else to live their Purpose fully.

CHAPTER 12

PUBLIC AND PRIVATE

ACCOUNTABLE PEOPLE KNOW how to harness the immense power of a Mission that inspires, engages, and motivates other people. The kind of Mission I am talking about is always rooted in some deeply personal motivation—some larger Purpose that drives everything in the leader's life. Yet as we saw in the previous chapter, this individual Purpose is a private matter. It is not necessarily what people buy into and sign on for when they support the Mission.

Articulating the right Mission and taking action on it in a way that attracts others to take it on are a big part of what makes someone an accountable person. Within your Accountability Circle, you must connect the dots and share how your Purpose supports your Mission. And if you are the leader of an organization, you must share with your Accountability Partners how your Purpose connects to the organizational Mission.[6]

---

6 Yes, this means you will need to repeat the process of creating a Mission Statement for your company or nonprofit, writing it in such a way that it directly expresses your *organizational* Mission, as opposed to your *personal* Mission (which you also need to get down in black and white). In many cases, these two Missions will be virtually identical. In my case, it was a matter of simply replacing the pronoun "I" with the pronoun "we." If you are the leader of an organization and you find that your organization's Mission Statement is wildly different from your personal Mission Statement, you may have a problem to solve. These two Narratives must align very closely. Both, of course, must express your Purpose in action. To find out how to get help on drafting an organizational Mission Statement that supports your Purpose, visit https://www.samsilverstein.com/connect/.

Outside of the Circle, however, you may well be looking at a situation where you opt to keep your Purpose entirely private. In fact, it may be easiest to win support for your Mission if you choose to focus publicly only on the Mission and not on the personal *Why* that powers it.

Let me share a real-life example with you that illustrates what I mean. There is an attorney based in St. Louis by the name of Jim Singer. I mention him because Jim is one of my favorite examples of a guy who literally became a man on a Mission.

Jim happened to come across the shameful true story of how a prominent, successful, and generous black ophthalmologist, Dr. H. Phillip Venable, was forbidden to occupy a home built on land that he owned in Creve Coeur, Missouri. This was back in the late 1950s; then, as now, Creve Coeur was an upscale suburb of St. Louis. City leaders of the period put up all kinds of dubious legal and administrative obstacles to the integration of their city; they eventually simply seized Venable's land, as well as that of eleven other black families who wanted to move into the elite, all-white neighborhood where they had purchased property. The pretext of the city leaders was that they wanted to build a park. Their real aim was to prevent African Americans from owning and living in homes in Creve Coeur.

A few years ago, Singer started doing some research about this sad episode, which was all too typical of the period. He was able to piece together the details of the story of how city leaders, notably the mayor of the town, John Beirne, pressured, humiliated, and intimidated the black families who owned property in Creve Coeur. Eventually, Singer began sharing this story with others and was able to paint a powerful picture of the extraordinary man in the middle of this controversy: of the twelve property owners in question, Venable alone opted to mount a legal challenge to the appropriation of his land by the city. He lost in court. The park was built and named after Mayor Beirne. And the Venables' home was repurposed as the park clubhouse.

Six decades later, Jim Singer decided that it was time to write a new ending to that story.

He launched a campaign to rename the park after Dr. Venable. That was his Mission. He had a clear objective, and he started designing and executing a definite plan of action in support of that objective.

Jim shared what he had learned with anyone who would listen. He wrote articles. He reached out to community leaders. He reached out to historical societies and universities. In short, he did everything he could to raise awareness about what had happened to the Venable family and about what he felt needed to happen next.

"It was the wrong thing then," he said of the successful efforts of racist city officials to exclude the Venables and the other black families from Creve Coeur. "And it is the wrong thing now."

He started out all alone in spreading that simple message and in advocating for a new name for the park. He was not alone for long, though. Hundreds of people, including my wife Renee and myself, eventually read his research and took an interest in the case, and the proposed name change for which he lobbied so tirelessly began to attract media attention. Renee and I were moved, along with hundreds of others, to show up at City Hall and speak out on this issue.

In late 2019, the Creve Coeur City Council voted unanimously to draft an ordinance that would officially change the name of the park from Beirne Park to H. Phillip Venable Memorial Park and in the process erect a plaque that would explain the story so that all who saw it could learn from the mistakes made in the past.

I have two big points to make here. First and foremost, I want you to notice that Jim Singer is a leader. This is not because of any position he occupies on any organizational chart but rather because of his ability to formulate and share *a compelling Mission that engages and attracts others.*

And second, I want you to notice that we really do not know what deep personal Purpose *motivated* Jim to do what he did. That is okay. And it may even be ideal. In a case like this, what matters most to those of us who choose to sign on is the Mission itself.

You and I do not have to know the closely held personal beliefs and standards that led Jim to advocate and engage with others about this particular issue. There might have been a personal spiritual or religious standard at the root of all this. It might have been something else entirely. From a practical point of view, however, it does not matter (to anyone but Jim) what those beliefs and standards are. What really matters is whether others bought into the Mission he was moved to articulate and whether they found themselves inspired enough to support that Mission in some way. Speaking for myself, I was! Getting involved with this Mission was an easy decision for me because it aligned with my personal Purpose and my Mission.

So this is a good time to start thinking about the following questions:

👉 What is your Mission? What is the clear objective, accompanied by a definite plan of action, that your own deep sense of Purpose now inspires you to pursue?

👉 How can you communicate that Mission to others in a way that engages them and motivates them to join your cause?

👉 What relational commitments are you willing to make, and keep, in order to fulfill that Mission?

Once you have the answers to these questions, you will be in a position to create a Mission that makes sense to you because it connects with your Purpose…and that also makes sense in the public sphere, when you share it with potential Allies.

>
>
> ## A MISSION WORKS IN TWO DIRECTIONS
>
> Create a Mission that makes sense to you because it connects with your Purpose...and that also makes sense in the public sphere, when you share it with potential Allies.

GAIN INSPIRATION FROM THE GREAT MISSIONS OF THE PAST

While we are on the topic of what happened in Creve Coeur as a result of Jim Singer's inspiring Mission there, let me point out that you will, from time to time, come across examples of people from history whose public commitment to their Mission inspires and informs your own Mission. For instance, as an Ally to Jim Singer's Mission, I ended up learning a great deal about the man at the center of the legal controversy back in the 1950s that gave rise to the whole renaming initiative: Dr. H. Phillip Venable. The more I learned about Dr. Venable's work, the more inspired I became about his life story, and the more committed I became to my own Mission. I began to suspect he had a powerful, visible, long-term Mission of his own, one that had to do with empowering people in his community.

Why do I say that? Because in addition to being the director of three ophthalmology departments, a researcher credited with numerous breakthroughs in his chosen field, and the first black member of the faculty at Washington University in St. Louis, Dr. Venable was deeply involved in supporting the careers, aspirations, and potential of people in the African-American community. He was a tireless recruiter of African-American medical students, he set up a major philanthropic initiative to benefit minority students of medicine, and he was the head of a hospital dedicated to serving low-income (and predominantly African-American) patients in St. Louis. The more closely you look at his life, the more obvious it becomes that he was deeply committed to a Mission of lifting up African Americans, often by inspiring them to create and capitalize on their own opportunities and serve their communities during a time of profound racial discrimination in this country—both structural/institutional and ideological.

After only a little time studying Dr. Venable's many contributions, I got a deeper sense of the kind of man he was—and the kind of person he inspired others to become. I also began to get a sense of the big *Why*—the Purpose—that seemed to motivate everything to which he devoted his energy. I believe he did what he did to empower African Americans at a time when there were many, many circumstances that disempowered them. I do not know that for sure, because he appears to have kept his Purpose to himself, as many great leaders do. But the public side of his leadership seems to align with that Purpose.

Take that legal dispute he ended up losing, for example. Notice that he was the only one committed to spending a significant amount of money, time, and attention on a case that he must have known had very little chance of succeeding. Do you think he did that because he wanted the personal satisfaction that would accompany a victory in court? I am sure he would have appreciated such a victory, but the more I learn about the man, the more convinced I am that he did what he did, not to pad his own ego, but to provide an example to others in his community. He was, I think, saying to them: "I am waging this battle, not because I think it will be won during my lifetime, but because it is the right thing to do. And I am challenging you to do the same in your time."

We are all familiar with the most famous Missions: President Kennedy's challenge to land a man on the moon and return him safely,

Dr. Martin Luther King's struggle to secure civil rights for all—not as a promise, but as a reality. These are indeed grand and inspiring Missions. But we can also be inspired on a personal level by the Missions of others who are less well known to history. For me, Dr. Venable was such a man on a Mission.

Dr. Venable is not a household name—at least not yet—but his story is an important one, because it shines a light on the extraordinary, enduring power of the right Mission. Here is someone from a time long past, someone who passed away years ago. His legacy, I believe, lies in the worthwhile Missions he has inspired, and is still inspiring, other people to take on. Jim Singer's, of course, is one of those, but there are doubtless many others.

Each of us, I believe, needs to find examples of such people—people whose Mission and whose personal example in pursuing that Mission inspire and motivate us in a personal and powerful way. I found Dr. Venable and was moved by his example for the simple reason that this was someone who made, and two decades after his passing continues to make, a huge positive difference in people's lives, who was not the head of a company, not a government official, and not a celebrity. That is inspiring to me personally, at a very deep level. My challenge to you is to find someone like Dr. Venable who inspires you in a similar way. There are thousands of people like that—people whose Mission is so powerful that it outlives them and continues to attract and inspire others. Find your own example! Then *become* someone like that! Identify your own Purpose and take action on it with an inspiring Mission of your own—a Mission that attracts, instructs, and inspires others!

LOOK TO HISTORY

 Find someone whose Mission is so powerful that it outlives them and continues to attract, instruct, and inspire others—including you.

Accountability Takeaways: Chapter 12

Be ready to ask yourself:

- What is my Mission? What is the clear objective, accompanied by a definite plan of action, that my own deep sense of Purpose now inspires me to pursue?

- How can I communicate that Mission to others in a way that engages them and motivates them to join this cause?

- What relational commitments am I willing to make, and keep, in order to fulfill this Mission?

Create a Mission that makes sense to you because it connects to your Purpose...and that also makes sense in the public sphere, when you share it with potential Allies.

Find someone whose Mission is so powerful that it outlives them and continues to attract, instruct, and inspire others—including you.

CHAPTER 13

SIX POWERFUL QUESTIONS ABOUT MISSION

AS I WAS WORKING on this book and sharing the key principles underlying a successful Mission with those in my own Accountability Circle, another extraordinary example from history kept presenting itself to me: that of President Franklin Delano Roosevelt when he took office back in 1933, perhaps the darkest year of the Great Depression. In his inaugural address, Roosevelt shared his Mission of putting Americans back to work. He said he aimed to do that by "engaging on a national scale" the most pressing economic challenges of the day. This was a remarkable moment. Up to that point in American history, the prevailing viewpoint of political leaders had been that the federal government should not directly intervene in economic affairs and that it had neither the ability nor the right to set up programs designed to provide jobs or economic relief to its citizens. Times, however, had changed. The question was, *how* would they change?

It is easy to lose sight, at this distance of years, of just how dire that economic crisis was that the United States (and the world) faced in the early months of 1933. This is not meant to be a book of history, but in order to give modern readers a little context, it is worth pausing a moment to point out, very briefly, what life looked like in the United States of America in the year that Roosevelt first took office.

The official national unemployment rate went into the books at 24.9 percent that year. In some parts of the country, notably the industrial Midwest, the unemployment rate was a staggering 36 percent. Nearly half of the country's banks had failed. A series of severe droughts in the Southern Plains had devastated agriculture from Texas to Nebraska, leading to economic disaster in many rural communities. This was the so-called Dust Bowl, a catastrophe that led to a mass migration of displaced people from ravaged farmlands, seeking work in cities that had no work to offer. We have seen nothing like 1933 in all the years since, thank goodness. It is no exaggeration to say that the country was teetering on the brink of economic and social collapse by the time Franklin Roosevelt took the oath of office.

I mention Roosevelt's Mission to put Americans back to work and the extraordinary obstacles he faced in pursuing that Mission for one simple reason: he took on a huge Mission, one that really mattered... without any clear sense of how, precisely, he was going to fulfill it.

THE FDR PRINCIPLE

 Take on a huge Mission that really matters... without any clear sense of how, precisely, you are going to fulfill it. The people and resources you need will present themselves when you make the decision to commit to the Mission. When you step through the door, people show up.

Nobody knew for sure what would reduce unemployment. Nobody knew for sure how to revive the seemingly moribund Dust Bowl. Roosevelt himself did not claim to know exactly what would bring about recovery.

During the campaign of the previous year, FDR had already clearly laid out his attitude toward the Mission he had taken: he would not pretend that he had all the answers. He would experiment. "The country needs," he said, "and, unless I mistake its temper, the country demands bold, persistent experimentation. It is common sense to take a method and try it: If it fails, admit it frankly and try another. But above all, try something."

In short, FDR promised to experiment until he found something that worked and to keep on experimenting to build on what worked. That is what leaders of a great Mission do. They know that if they wait until they have all the answers to take action, the Mission will fail. And in 1933, there was no room for error. The Mission could not fail. Someone in Roosevelt's entourage remarked, before Inauguration Day, that if Roosevelt succeeded, he would go down in history as the greatest American president. "If I fail," Roosevelt said, "I'll go down in history as the last American president."

He was not the last president. I share his story and his mindset of "take a method and try it" because it is a great and enduring example for all of us who aspire to a Mission worthy of our Purpose. You can expect such a Mission to take you out of your comfort zone. You can expect it to demand that you take it on *before* you have all the Allies, all the resources, all the ideas you will need. The magic of the Mission lies in the decision to gain clarity and take action without those things. FDR released himself to his Mission without knowing how he would pull it off. In fact, he released himself to it during the campaign, before he even reached the White House! This chapter of the book will show you how to release yourself to your own Mission.

Clarifying your Mission and releasing yourself to it requires a self-assessment, just as clarifying your Purpose does. The six questions below will take some time and effort to answer, but they are well worth the investment, because they will point you toward the creation of your own Mission Narrative...and give you the kind of clarity FDR had about getting America back to work.

Be prepared to create *written* answers to each of the six questions.

Question One:
What Is Your Purpose?

Go back to the work you did in Chapters 6–10 and review the concise Statement of Purpose you came up with there. Tweak it and refine it if that is appropriate, but make sure it is still a *concise* statement of the big *Why* that drives you and connects you to the larger world.

As you read these questions, feel free to go back and review my Purpose (see Chapter 6) and my Mission Narrative (see Chapter 11), which you can use as a model for your own. Do not try to use my Mission Narrative as your own...but do look at it as an example of what should go where.

Question Two:
Whom Have You Helped Joyfully, and What Were You Doing When You Helped Them?

Get specific. Take some time. Think of particular people, places, and situations. I recommend taking at least a half an hour to jot down particular examples of joyous service in your life.

Question Three:
What Is Your Mission?

Draft a single sentence that reflects the ACTION side of your Purpose. This is your Mission. Remember, your Purpose and your Mission are two sides of the same coin. Your Mission is your Purpose in action.

Question Four:
How Do You Apply Your Purpose Right Now?

What specific actions do you take that support your stated Purpose? Make a written list of the verbs that capture the DOING aspect of your Purpose in your current experience.

Question Five:
How Could You Apply Your Purpose in the Future?

What specific actions do you want to take, but have not yet taken, that would support your stated Purpose? Make a written list of the verbs that capture the DOING aspect of your Purpose in the future that you most want to live.

Question Six:
What Three Activities That Connect *Directly* to Your Mission Bring You the Most Joy When You Think about Them?

Review the lists of verbs you have written down in response to questions four and five and select the three that make you feel the most excited the instant that you read them. These three verbs should support your Purpose. Then write a sentence or two about each that clarifies what that verb means to you in practical terms. Taken together with your Mission, this forms your Mission Narrative.

Accountability Takeaways: Chapter 13

To identify your Mission and create a powerful Mission Narrative, ask yourself these questions:

- What is my Purpose?

- Whom have I helped joyfully, and what was I doing when I helped them?

- What is my Mission?

- How do I apply my Purpose right now?

- How could I apply my Purpose in the future?

- What three activities that connect directly to my Mission bring me the most joy when I think about them?

CHAPTER 14

ACCOUNTABILITY
AND VALUES

YOUR VALUES EMBODY your principles and your standards of behavior—what is important in your life. They are the *How*.

WHAT ARE VALUES?

Your Values state your principles and your standards of behavior—what is important in your life. They are the HOW.

A Value is something that is extremely important to you. It is so important that if you lost it, you would move heaven and earth looking for it. That is why we call it a Value. You value it.

Your Values are your House Rules. They help you clarify the answers to important questions, such as:

 What do I believe?

 How do I act when no one is looking?

 How do we act in this family?

👉 How do we act on this team?

👉 How do we act in this company?

👉 and so on.

Values determine how we see, connect to, and treat other people. They are the foundation for the relationships we build with the people in our world.

Your House Rules are always your House Rules. They apply everywhere, all the time. As an accountable person, you cannot have one set of rules for public display and another set of rules for everyday life and decision-making. You either live the Values or you do not.

One of the main reasons to join an Accountability Circle is to get direct, immediate feedback from people you trust implicitly who will tell you when you are not living the Values that you say are yours.

Yes, there are going to be times when you slip up. You are human. But it is important to understand the two different ways that people tend to slip up when it comes to Values.

If you *inadvertently* make a decision that does not align with your Values, you need to notice it, acknowledge what happened, and fix it fast. I call this Situation One. An Accountability Circle relationship will help you get into the habit of dealing with this situation directly and immediately.

On the other hand, if you have a pattern of making a decision that *purposely* violates a stated core Value—meaning you know full well that a given decision will violate the core Value you say you have, and you consistently make that decision anyway—then *you do not have that Value.* You are not living it, *period.* And your Accountability Partner has an obligation to tell you that.

This is Situation Two, and it is a sign of a deep problem. If you want to start living the Value, you need to start making different choices and start holding yourself to a different standard. Notice that in this situation, I am not talking about times when you slipped away from the Value in the heat of the moment without meaning to. What I am talking about is a pattern of conscious choices, a recurrent pattern of behavior, that undermines the person you claim to be. This is considerably worse than having no stated Values at all.

Let me give you a practical example of what I am talking about so that you can easily see the difference between the two situations.

Suppose you are the owner of a company, and suppose you have publicly adopted, both for yourself and for the organization as a whole, the Value of *Respect.*

And suppose that you have taken the time and effort to break down, for yourself and everyone in your organization, exactly what you mean by Respect. You have made sure that the following text appears on posters in your breakroom, all your onboarding materials, and all your human resource materials:

> We respect each other, our customers, our suppliers, and all of our stakeholders. If there is a problem, we go to the person or people involved and we address the issues professionally and directly. We do not talk behind people's backs, and we do not make disparaging or demeaning comments about others. We assume good intent in others, and we focus on the possible.

Now, what you have just read is an important early step. It is a good, concise summary of what the value Respect actually means to a given person and a given workplace. You do need something like that in writing so that everyone has a good idea of what kinds of behavior the Value supports—and does not support. (By the way, this is just one example of how an organization could go about defining Respect; each organization must create a viable definition for itself. There is no one authoritative definition.)

Notice, though, that what you post about Respect in the breakroom, talk about with regard to Respect during onboarding, and include about Respect in your HR binders is essentially *meaningless* without actions that support Respect.

So now let's look at our two situations.

It is the end of a very long day, and you and your team have been working on a complex, demanding project. One of your employees, Jerry, has made an unfortunate error that went undetected until the last minute. Jerry has gone home early. No one else can fix the problem caused by Jerry's error. No one can reach Jerry by phone or text; he seems to have turned off his phone. You are in limbo: you have missed your deadline. This project was supposed to wrap up today, but with Jerry unavailable it turns out that there is no way it can be completed until tomorrow. You are frustrated. While the rest of your team members are in your office, you say, "That is just like Jerry to leave early without checking with anyone. He is so unreliable. I cannot believe I trusted him to pull his weight. He is an amateur. This episode proves it."

In Situation One, you immediately realize that you have just stepped outside of the Value of Respect. Because you know that your actions and decisions in relation to Values determine whether the company as a whole upholds the stated Value, you apologize to the team and, at the first opportunity, to Jerry. You say something like, "I am really sorry, everyone. It has been a long day, and I really wanted to get this project finished this afternoon, but that is no excuse for speaking disrespectfully about Jerry or talking about him behind his back. That is not how we operate here. We will pick this up tomorrow, and I will let Jerry know that I made this mistake and apologize to him." Notice that this apology is a *decision*. More specifically, it is a decision that aligns with the Value of Respect.

In Situation Two, you make an excuse, and you do not say anything to the team, or to Jerry, about having ignored the stated Value that supposedly defines you and your business. You make sure the excuse you tell yourself sounds convincing. Very often, such excuses are built around the word *but*. For instance: "I know what I said was not in keeping with the Value of Respect, *but*...this was a very important project, and Jerry should have known better than to leave early without telling anyone how to reach him. This was a special circumstance." Notice that making an excuse is also a *decision*, one that does *not* align with the Value of Respect. Such decisions are particularly damaging when they are made by a leader. This kind of decision-making is like an addictive drug. It is habit-forming. It becomes a pattern.

In Situation Two, we habitually identify the choices we make that ignore our stated Values as "special circumstances," and we teach everyone else to do the same. Actions really do speak louder than words. Pretty soon, "special circumstances" are how we and everyone else around us actually operates day in and day out. We all get used to making excuses for behavior that runs contrary to the very Values we say are important to us. *Which means they are not important to us.*

Stated Values have no meaning unless our actions align with those Values in the decisions that we make. Only when our actions align with our Values are the Values truly ours.

A CONTINUOUS CONVERSATION

 The Accountability Circle is complete only if it encompasses a continuous conversation of how the stated Values of each Accountability Partner align with their actions.

BEYOND THE LIES

In Situation One, we are well positioned to share our stated Values with others, ideally by means of our actions, but if necessary also by means of our words.

In Situation Two, we are *not* well positioned to do any of that. Why not? Because we are liars, pure and simple. Any attempt we make to promote, support, or implement the stated Values that we habitually betray is going to be both morally and practically compromised because those attempts will be based on falsehood. If we say we have a Value but our actions do not align with our words, we do not have that Value. It is that simple.

Where there are lies, there can be no accountability. Who wants to work for, or with, a liar? Who wants to build their life around such a person?

If we are not willing to admit what is really going on when we lie to ourselves and others about our Values, then we are part of the problem and not part of the solution. When we lie about our Values, we may not even realize that that is what we are doing. We may be lying to ourselves, as well! (Human beings are good at that.) This is why we must rely on our Accountability Partners to call us on this when they see a disconnect about Values happening. Whenever they do, we are obliged not only to listen, but also to change our life so that it is based on Values we are willing to actually uphold.

WHY LIES ABOUT VALUES HAPPEN

Usually, people lie about their Values because they have followed the common pattern of (publicly) adopting a certain Value without stopping to consider whether or not the Value in question is truly important to them. The Value that comes out of their mouth is not what they believe. Remember: A Value is something that is so important to you that you move heaven and earth to restore it if you happen to lose it.

Sometimes, people start talking about a given Value because they think doing so makes them look good, or because they think it is what a particular individual wants to hear, or because some other person or organization publicly adopted the Value and they want to be like that person or organization. This kind of Value is pasted on from the outside. It has nothing to do with the individual proclaiming it. It is what the person thinks is *supposed* to be important, not what actually *is* important.

People with Accountability Partners do not fall into this trap. They follow a process that helps them identify the *right* Values, the Values that are true to them as individuals, Values that they can and do align with. This takes a little time. Once you have invested the time and identified such Values, once you have begun living them—not before—you can discuss them with your Accountability Partner, share them with others, and perhaps build a team and an organization around them. In Chapter 17, I will be sharing a process I have been using for years with my clients that will help you identify the Values that truly are important to you as a person.

HOW NOT TO SELECT VALUES

 Never select a Value to live by because you think you are supposed to. Select a Value to live by because it is important to you personally—because it is true to who you are, it is what you believe, it is rooted in truth, it respects the rights of others, and it is what you are willing to honor in your actions and choices.

For the sake of example and to give you a point of reference, I have reproduced my own list of Values below. These Values have been discovered and refined over time using the very same process I will be sharing with you a little later in this book. Notice that like the Mission, the Value Statement takes the form of a narrative expanding on three carefully chosen words. Notice, too, that each of these words describes something that is of vital importance to me personally. *You will have to identify and unpack your own Values. Do not try to use mine verbatim!* That would defeat the whole purpose of what we are doing, which is to identify what is vitally important to YOU as an individual.

My Values:

INTEGRITY

I make decisions based on the belief that my word is my bond and doing what is right is always the right thing to do. I commit to this no matter what.

RESPECT

I see all people as equal. I value other people's opinions, appreciate their beliefs, and recognize the importance of their priorities.

SIGNIFICANCE

I create meaning in my life and the lives of the people around me. I look for ways to create significance for my family. I make the effort to get to know people. I look for potential in the people with whom I come in contact. I encourage people. I participate in my community and work to make a difference.

Life is an adventure. I actively live that adventure when I live with integrity, respect, and significance.

"Be strong and resolute."

There is nothing magical about my expression of Values, only something pragmatic. What I mean is that this Value Narrative works for me. The big question is not, "How can you adopt these specific Values?" but rather, "What works for you?" That is what we are here to find out.

Accountability Takeaways: Chapter 14

Your Values state your principles and your standards of behavior—what is important in your life. They are the **How**.

The Accountability Circle is complete only if it encompasses a continuous conversation of how the stated Values of each Accountability Partner align with their actions.

Never select a Value to live by because you think you are supposed to. Select a Value to live by because it is important to you personally—because it is true to who you are, it is what you believe, it is rooted in truth, it respects the rights of others, and it is what you are willing to honor in your actions and choices.

CHAPTER 15

WHY BOTHER
WITH VALUES?

FOR MANY OF US, our only direct contact with the concept of Values comes at work, and it is not a positive point of contact.

We see a sentence printed in big letters on the onboarding manual or posted on our breakroom wall that says something along the lines of, "At MassiveCorp, our values are quality, integrity, and safety." Then we get a news alert on our phone that says, "The MassiveCorp CEO has just resigned following a scandal involving a cover-up of product safety concerns raised by employees on the production line. Federal investigators are considering issuing an indictment against the executive."

And we think, "So much for quality, integrity, and safety." We think, "Why even bother putting together a list of Values? That's what hypocrites do."

Whose fault is it that we feel that way? Leadership's. All too often, our leadership has failed us. Is it any wonder people get jaded about the whole idea of Values? Is it any wonder they show up at work for the sole objective of collecting a paycheck?

I want to take a very different approach. I want you to forget everything you think you know about Values. I want to take you back to the *Orca*, back to that boat that Brody, Quint, and Hooper have just boarded in support of a powerful, inspiring Mission: *kill the shark.* And I want to ask you a very important question: *What do we know about these guys?*

Well, we know that the Mission they have undertaken is the active expression of Brody's Purpose: *to protect people.* And we also know that Quint and Hooper have been attracted to and signed on to that Mission because they each have a Mission of their own that, while not identical to Brody's, aligns with his.

What we do not yet know is *how* they will be taking on that Mission as a team, what House Rules they will be following. And to figure that out, we need to look at what makes Police Chief Martin Brody tick. We need to figure out what is most important to him. In short, we need to figure out what his Values are.

VALUES IN A NUTSHELL

 Your Values are what make you tick. When you figure out what is most important to you, you figure out your Values.

Notice that even though it is Quint who is the undisputed captain of the boat, we are interested here in what makes *Brody* tick. Why? Because this is Brody's Mission and because Brody has chosen the Allies who will help him attain his goals. We must not be misled by the role that Quint plays on the team. Even though the *Orca* is Quint's boat, this is Brody's journey. Because Brody has selected the team and because he has set the criteria for success, he is ultimately responsible for the outcome of the operation. Quint acknowledges as much when he gives Brody his nickname, "Chief." So we want to look closely at the

House Rules that Brody sets for himself and lives by, and we want to explore how those House Rules impact his Allies and his Mission.

What can we say is truly most important to Brody during this Mission, as evidenced by his actions? It is what we actually *do* that makes a difference in terms of our Values; that is far more important than what we say. There are, as I see it, three major things to consider here.

Courage. Brody is willing to move beyond what is comfortable and familiar to him and to face down the unknown, despite the very natural feelings of fear and anxiety that accompany him on this voyage. He hates boats, hates the open water, and has a lifelong fear of drowning, due to trauma he experienced as a child. He sets all of that aside. Courage, we should remember, is not the quality of feeling zero fear. It is the quality of feeling fear and *taking action anyway.* Brody knew when he stepped onto the Orca that he was confronting a predator quite capable of killing him and his companions. He took action anyway and agreed to serve as a member of the crew. This value of Courage turns out to be absolutely essential to the fulfillment of the Mission. As new challenges emerge, new fears have to be confronted and left behind if he is to fulfill his Purpose. It is a sign of his good judgment that the two Allies he has chosen sense the Courage Brody shows at the outset and easily accept the Value of Courage as a prerequisite of the Mission. Note that whenever you hire someone, you want to see clear evidence of action that supports *your* Values in *their* past. It is that action that shows that your Values already exist in who they are.

Respect. Brody, like a lot of great leaders, has deep respect for people who know how to do important jobs that he himself does not know how to do. For instance, Brody has no idea how to find a great white shark; Hooper does. Brody respects him for that ability and treats him accordingly, never micromanaging or challenging him in any area where it is obvious that Hooper knows more than he does.

Similarly, Brody does not know port from starboard or bow from stern as the journey begins and has no idea how to captain a boat. Quint does know how to captain a boat, and Brody shows him immense Respect for this skill. It is easy to lose sight of how important Brody's quiet example of Respect for these two men is to the Mission that is the heart of the story. At the beginning of the voyage, Quint is riding Hooper pretty hard and is constantly making insulting remarks about his small crew; Hooper, unlike Brody, clearly resents this, and he gripes about Quint when he thinks the captain cannot hear. Brody models the Value of Respect for both of his shipmates, keeping his head down, doing his work, and avoiding all opportunities to snipe at the skipper. This choice to *live and model* the Value of Respect allows him to serve as a kind of bridge between the two very different men he has recruited as Allies and eventually makes possible a cohesion that otherwise would have been very difficult to attain. Brody's personal commitment to the Value of Respect makes him the glue that holds the little team together. The personal Respect I am talking about is confirmed and strengthened in the scene where the three men compare their wounds and scars. Keep an eye out for it the next time you watch the film. In the meantime, consider the possibility that because of Brody's quiet decision to live the Value of Respect, to give Respect before he expects to receive it in return, Brody is able to ensure it becomes a House Rule. The Mission would be doomed without it.

Truth and Integrity. Brody tells the truth, he does what he says he is going to do, and he is committed to doing the right thing. Truth and Integrity matter to him. That does not mean he never makes mistakes. It does not mean that he never has conflicts. But it does mean that he is a straight shooter, he has a clear sense of right and wrong, and he keeps his promises. When Brody agrees to follow orders on the boat, he makes good on that important commitment because he believes it is the right thing to do. In doing so, he serves as an important role model for Hooper. That kind of commitment to Integrity is vitally important in a life-or-death situation, and of course it is vitally important in everyday life, too. Brody knows there is no room for dishonesty or evasion on this Mission: fortunately, both the men he has recruited also know that, and they too are driven by Truth and Integrity. They follow through on what they say they will do, they tell each other the truth, and they strive to do the right thing as they see it.

What I have just given you is an extended Values Narrative that matches up with the Values set of the leader who undertook the Mission of killing the shark in the film *Jaws*. What mattered most to Brody as the leader of the Mission were three big things: Courage, Respect, and Truth and Integrity. These were not simply slogans that Brody recited. They were *actions*. They were *what he insisted on in his relationships*. This is Brody's Value Set, which both of his Allies bought into, based on his personal example.

LIVE THE VALUES

When we choose Allies, we must be absolutely certain that they are living the Values of the organization. And the only effective way to do this is to start by living those Values ourselves!

Brody's adherence to these three Values—Courage, Respect, Truth/Integrity—and his actions in support of them position him as the kind of leader I would want to follow. But suppose someone on the boat had rejected those Values? Suppose one of the men on that boat had never moved out of his comfort zone on anything of consequence and had no desire to do so now? Suppose he had been frozen with fear at the moment when his companions needed him the most? Suppose one of the men had no particular inclination to respect others or be respected in turn? Suppose one of the men had been a habitual liar?

That man would have been a threat to the Mission. And he would not have belonged on the boat. His habitual actions, which reveal his Values, would have conflicted with Brody's Values.

> ## BE CAREFUL WHO YOU LET ON THE BOAT
>
> When it becomes clear that someone is consistently failing to live the Values you have established for your team, company, or organization, that person should not be allowed on the "boat."

The Allies with whom we work to support our Mission may not buy into our Purpose and may not even know what that Purpose is. That is fine. But if they have a Value Set that habitually takes actions that *conflict* with our Values and our Purpose, we have to part company with them. Not only that—if we *know* that their actions habitually conflict with our Purpose, we must not make Allies of them in the first place.

What do you do, though, if there is a situation where someone who is already on your "boat" takes an action that clearly counters your Value—by, for instance, speaking disrespectfully to a colleague? In that case, if you are the leader, it is your job both to engage with that person privately and tactfully so that you can reinforce what the organizational Values are and also to make sure you *model* the Value properly in your interactions with that team member and everyone else. Then you keep a watchful eye. If the pattern repeats itself, you make it clear—again, privately and tactfully—that upholding the

Value in question is a precondition of being a member of the team. If the pattern still continues, you part company. This person has to go find another "boat" to be on. Yours is not an option. Any other path undermines accountability. If a person consistently rejects the team's Values and you keep that person on, what you are really saying to the rest of the team is that you have *no* Values! That's not the message you want to send.

A SPECIAL NOTE ON INTEGRITY

If you try to create a Values Narrative that does not begin from a place of Integrity—which I define as doing what you know is right, regardless of whether anyone else notices—then the entire exercise of creating a Values Narrative will be a waste of time.

Integrity is non-negotiable. Regardless of whether you include it in your Values Narrative, it has to be present. You have to be committed to doing what you know is right, and you have to mean it when you make that commitment. If Integrity is not something you are willing to build your life around, something you are willing to take action to restore the minute you notice that you have lost sight of it, then there is really no point in taking part in an Accountability Circle at all. This whole undertaking has Integrity at its foundation. If you ignore that fact, accountability will be absent from your life and your Accountability Circle will fail.

REAL INTEGRITY IS NON-NEGOTIABLE

"Real integrity is doing the right thing, knowing that nobody's going to know whether you did it or not." —Oprah Winfrey

Fortunately, Integrity is a foundational human value. By that I mean it is already central to our relationships and to any worthy undertaking. Whether we choose to embrace it in words or not, we all know that we are supposed to do the right thing, even when the right thing is not easy or popular or convenient. If we have a problem with that, we should ask ourselves why that is.

While I never advise a client on what specific words need to show up in the Values Narrative, I will tell you that Integrity is at the heart of all we are doing here, regardless of the Values you select for the Narrative.

Accountability Takeaways: Chapter 15

Your Values are what make you tick. When you figure out what is most important to you, you figure out your Values.

When we choose Allies, we must be absolutely certain that they are living the Values of the organization. And the only effective way to do this is to start by living those Values ourselves!

When it becomes clear that someone is consistently failing to live the Values, that person should not be allowed on the "boat" of your team, company, or organization.

Real Integrity—doing the right thing whether anyone is watching or not—is non-negotiable.

CHAPTER 16

TWO TRUE STORIES
ABOUT VALUES

IN BELFAST, NORTHERN IRELAND, there is a supermarket checkout clerk by the name of David Vance. Vance works for a grocery chain known as Lidl, which is one of the major players in the UK and Irish markets. One day, in the autumn of 2019, Vance was on duty, doing his job at the "till," checking out customers, when he noticed that the elderly man at the front of the line was having some trouble with his credit card. The man tried using the card once. It did not go through. He tried using it a second time. It did not go through. Vance noticed that this customer was starting to get a little stressed. It was at that point that he did something most checkout clerks do not and would not even think to do…

He quietly paid for the customer's groceries.

Vance did not even inform the elderly gentleman of what he had done. He was not looking for credit. He simply spotted a customer in distress, assessed the situation, made the payment, and let the customer walk away believing that some kind of technical problem had arisen and had then been addressed.

CONTRIBUTION IN ACTION

This story is all about the Value known as Contribution—not just words about Contribution, but actions that support Contribution. Words about what we Value are meaningless without action, and words are not any part of Vance's story. In fact, after he paid for those groceries, *Vance did not tell anyone what he had done.* The only way the larger world came to know of this event was through a Facebook post from another customer who observed Vance, thought his action was worthy of note, and said so online. The post got wide exposure and led to a popular piece in *Inc. Magazine.* He ended up being named Lidl's "Customer Service Champion of the Month."

VALUES ARE ALL ABOUT YOUR ACTIONS

Words about what we value are meaningless without action.

Of the recognition he received, Vance said simply, "I didn't think I did anything out of the ordinary." I have noticed that this is the outlook of a lot of people who have made a habit of contributing to the community. For Vance, the "community" is the store and its customers. It may at some point go further than that, of course, but that is the community he has supported and contributed to. We know that by his *actions,* not just by what he says.

Now, why do I tell you this story? Does Vance's example mean that every time a customer has a payment problem, the cashier is supposed to pay for the groceries? Of course not. What I want you to notice is that Vance acted with kindness and empathy *when he did not think anyone was watching.* That is an essential requirement of a functional core Value: it guides you even when there is zero social capital to be gained by supporting the Value.

If I were to ask David Vance what one of his core Values was, and he was to tell me, *"I take opportunities to make important contributions to the community in which I live. I give in a way that benefits others, whether they are close to me or not,"* I would have a definite reason to believe him. This would not just be something he says. There is action backing up his words. He owns that Value. It is a Value that connects him to his community. If David were to put this Value into writing, the act of writing it down would *not* be what made the Value his. Contribution is *already* a Value of his because he is already living it!

I have shared David Vance's example because I wanted you to get a clear idea of what living this Value looks like at the *individual* level—one person making a Contribution to his community. It is entirely possible, though, that someone who has taken on this Value could choose to express it on a far broader scale because of a strong personal sense that it is the right thing to do and because of differences in personal circumstances. That kind of expression of the Value would not make Vance's contribution less important; it is all a question of what your capacity, your experience, and your Mission is. Vance's contribution was totally appropriate and totally valid in his world, given his resources, his situation, and his opportunities. Let's continue, though, by taking a look at someone with the opportunity to live that exact same Value at a different scale, a scale that is appropriate in *his* world.

"WHERE IS THAT SHOWING UP?"

Robert Smith is the founder of Vista Equity Partners, an investment firm. His personal financial worth is estimated at approximately five billion dollars. Now, let's pretend that I am having a conversation with Mr. Smith, and I ask him what his core Values are. And let's assume he says to me that one of his core Values is Contribution, and specifically contribution to the community in which he lives. When I hear this, I might say (as I have said to any number of people over the years), "That's great! Just out of curiosity…where is that showing up in your life?"

And suppose that in my conversation with Mr. Smith, he answers by saying, "Well, the other day, I spotted an elderly gentleman at the checkout line at a grocery store who was having problems with his credit card. He kept swiping it, and it kept getting declined. Very tactfully, without making a fuss, I gave the young man at the cash register a twenty-dollar bill and made it clear that I wanted to pay for the elderly man's groceries. I left before the elderly man knew what I had done."

I might say in response, "That is wonderful! I am sure that must have made you feel great. Can you think of anything else you have done that supports the same Value?"

And suppose Mr. Smith thought for a long moment, scratched his head, then looked at me and said, "Nope. That's it."

Given that Mr. Smith has a personal net worth of five billion dollars, could he really say that he consistently lives the Value of contributing to the community? I doubt it. The best he could say would be that he *once* made a step in that direction.

Now, I am having a little bit of fun with this example, and I suspect you can see where I am going with all this. Let me share with you what Robert Smith *actually* did to fulfill his commitment to this Value.

In May of 2019, as he gave the commencement address at Morehouse University, Smith announced that his family was taking on the responsibility of *paying 100 percent of the student loan debt of the graduating class at Morehouse,* a historically black educational institution located in Atlanta. The payoff, which includes loans taken out by the students' parents or guardians, ended up costing Smith and his family $34 million. More than 400 Morehouse graduates had their loan debt completely erased.

In making his announcement, Smith made it clear that he was paying off the debts in the expectation that the members of the graduating class he was addressing would find a way to make a similar contribution of their own at some point down the line. "Now, I know my class will make sure they pay this forward," he told the stunned, happy students. "I want my class to look at these [alumni]—these beautiful Morehouse brothers—and let's make sure every class has the same opportunity going forward, because we are enough to take care of our own community. We are enough to ensure we have all the opportunities of the American dream."

In other words, Smith was not just making a contribution to this limited group. He wanted his contribution to lead to similar contributions in years to come, long after he has passed away. Notice that even though Smith (unlike Vance) chose to make his gift public, he did so for a specific reason: he wanted to inspire other philanthropists to follow his example, and he wanted to start a national conversation about reducing or eliminating student debt. So he is clearly thinking in the long term, both in terms of the message he sent to, and the example he set for, those 2019 Morehouse graduates, and in terms of his peers in the world of business and education. So him taking public "credit" for the gift is very much *in support of the core Value of Contribution to the community.*

Notice too that for Smith, the "community" is the entire universe of people who might go to college in the United States of America. That his definition of "community" is different from Vance's does not make him right and Vance wrong. They have each defined the word according to their own perspective and their own situation. *It is up to each of us to define what our Values mean and then to live up to what we have defined.*

IT IS UP TO YOU

It is up to each of us to define what our Values mean and then to live up to what we have defined.

A glimpse of what the Value of Contribution to the larger community means to Robert Smith can be found in something else he said to that group of graduating students: "Success is only real if our community is protected, our potential is realized, and if our most valuable assets—our people—find strength in owning the businesses that provide economic stability in our community." I think we also begin to get a sense of Robert Smith's personal Mission in those words, as well. When you spend enough time with accountable people, one of the things you notice about them is that their Purpose, their Mission, and their core Values are *all* visible in their actions.

For the record, this massive, purposeful financial gift is not a fluke. Mr. Smith, whom *Forbes* magazine has called the wealthiest African American in the United States, has made similarly substantial donations to other educational institutions, to arts causes, and to cancer research.

So, if I were to ask Robert Smith what one of his core Values was and if he were to tell me, *"I take opportunities to make important contributions to the community in which I live. I give in a way that benefits others, whether they are close to me or not,"* I would have substantial reason to believe him. This would not just be something he says. There would be action backing up his words. He clearly owns that Value.

Both of these examples are *equally* important and instructive. If you find yourself in Vance's situation and you claim Contribution as one of your community Values, do what he did: *live the Value!* Live the Value of Contribution at your level of ability. Do not be one of those people who talks the talk but fails to walk the walk. And similarly, if you are fortunate enough to operate at a higher financial level on a day-to-day basis, follow Robert Smith's example: *live the Value!*

LIVE YOUR VALUES

Live your Values...at your level of ability. Do not be one of those people who talks the talk but fails to walk the walk.

These examples use Contribution as the Value, but the same decision to take action applies to *all* of your Values. If you act on your Values, if they are showing up in your life or in your business, then the Value is real. It is that simple.

My point is, talk is cheap. If all you have is talk, and there is nothing that aligns with any commitment you make in support of your core Values, and talk is all that happens in your Accountability Circle, *you are not an accountable person.* Do what you can—*all* you can—with what you have right now. Take *action* on your Values. Make sure your Values actually show up in your life!

Accountability Takeaways: Chapter 16

Words about what we value are meaningless without action.

It is up to each of us to define what our Values mean and then to live up to what we have defined.

Live your Values…at your level of ability. Do not be one of those people who talks the talk but fails to walk the walk.

CHAPTER 17

SIX POWERFUL
QUESTIONS ABOUT VALUES

A FEW MONTHS AGO, a friend of mine whom I will call Eric and I were sharing coffee at a café. Eric started complaining about a mutual acquaintance whom I will call Leo.

A little background is in order here. Eric and Leo had once been close friends, but they had had a big argument and Eric had not moved past it. He was now holding a grudge, and he was taking advantage of the fact that Leo was not present. He went on a long diatribe against Leo, expecting me to agree with, or at least silently acquiesce in, all the bad things he had to say about his former friend: *Leo was irresponsible. Leo could not be trusted. Leo took unfair advantage of people.* On and on it went. At first, I held my tongue, hoping that the monologue would stop without me having to say anything. It did not. After about five minutes of this, I finally said:

"Eric, stop. Listen to me. This man used to be a friend of yours. Look at what you are doing now: talking about him behind his back, making all kinds of accusations about him when he is in no position to respond to them or defend himself. We both know that the way to handle a complaint is to take it to someone who can do something about it, and Eric, we both know I am not that person. Leo is. Now, I have known you for a long time. I know you and Leo have had your problems. But what I have to say to you now has zero to do with Leo and everything to do with you, and I hope you will take it in the spirit in which I intend it: *You are better than this,* and I think you know that."

The moment I spoke those words "You are better than this," something very interesting happened: Eric stopped himself cold. The monologue against his former friend was over. He looked at me, not as though I had caught him doing something he should not have been doing, but as though *he* had caught himself doing something that he should not have been doing.

I honestly do not know whether Eric and Leo ever settled their differences. I do know that Eric never went into backbiting mode again, at least in front of me. At that moment, with my forceful reminder that *he was better than this,* I had tapped into something important that he already knew about himself. He knew that what he was doing did not match up with his core Values.

A clear set of Values must do for you what I did for Eric at that moment. It must look you in the eyes at the moment of decision, the moment you are tempted to take a course of action that is contrary to who you really are, and it must tell you, in a way that stops you cold, *You are better than this.* And it must inspire you to correct your course.

The six powerful questions that follow will help you to create a Value set that does for you what my question did for Eric.

VALUES LET YOU COURSE CORRECT

A clear set of Values must look you in the eyes at the moment of decision, the moment you are tempted to take a course of action that is contrary to who you really are, and tell you, in a way that stops you cold, *You are better than this.*

SIX QUESTIONS ABOUT VALUES

Determining your personal Values, and creating a personal Values Narrative, is one of the very best investments you can make in yourself. Once you have written down the answers to the questions about your Purpose and your Mission, I strongly urge you to take the time to complete your work by following the process laid out here. Using this process, which I have developed over a series of years, shared with countless clients, and used myself, will help you avoid the common pitfall of writing down Values that "sound good" but do not stick.

Question One:
Who Are Your Heroes?

On a separate sheet of paper, I want you to write down the names of five of your Heroes. These should be people who have inspired you and made you think, "Hey, I really want to be like that person." You may have known them personally; you may not have. The people on your list could be living or dead. They could be fictional or real. All that matters is that the person is someone you admire deeply, someone whose example has made a difference for you and who has emerged as a role model.

So for example, you might list the following people on your list:

 Abraham Lincoln

 My Grandfather

 Spider-Man's Uncle Ben

 Marie Curie

 Martin Luther King

Question Two:
Why Are Those People Your Heroes?

Next to each of those names you just listed, I want you to write at least five words or brief phrases that describe specific personal qualities or traits that made you choose that person for your list. So for instance, if Lincoln was one of your Heroes and you were personally inspired by his quote "I am not bound to win, but I am bound to be true; I am not bound to succeed, but I am bound to live up to what light I have," then you might lead your list with the word Integrity. Your full list for Lincoln might look like this:

Abraham Lincoln:

 Integrity

 Committed to His Cause

 Eloquent

 Kept Things Together No Matter What

 Strong in Adversity

 Wise

 Saw the Big Picture

Do this for all five names on your list. Again, notice that even though you never knew Lincoln personally or never could know Spider-Man's Uncle Ben in real life, you *can* identify the ways of acting, thinking, communicating, and making decisions they displayed that have had a positive impact on you—the traits of theirs that have made you think, "I want to be like that."

The words you list for each figure should answer the question: *Why them?*

When you get done with Question Two, you should have at least *twenty-five* qualities listed—at least five for each person you have chosen.

Question Three:
Where Are You Right Now in Relation to Their Qualities?

For *each* of the qualities you have listed, I want you to honestly state where you are right now in your life with regard to living that quality, on a scale of one to ten. Be tough on yourself here. The only person who will read this sheet is *you*. Give yourself an accurate assessment in each area. Understand that a score of 10/10 means you never deviate from the highest standard set by your Hero in that area.

Ask yourself, in every area where you do not give yourself a 10 out of 10, why you gave yourself the score you did and what you would need to do to reach a score of 10 out of 10. (This part of the exercise can be the focus of a later discussion you have with your Accountability Partners.)

Once you have done that, I want you to underline the *one* quality for each Hero that you *most* wish you had in your life.

Your list for Lincoln might now look like this:

Abraham Lincoln:

 <u>Integrity (7/10)</u>

👍 Committed to His Cause (6/10)

👍 Eloquent (7/10)

👍 Kept Things Together No Matter What (8/10)

👍 Strong in Adversity (6/10)

👍 Wise (6/10)

👍 Saw the Big Picture (6/10)

Question Four:
What Are the Five Qualities You Have Underlined?

Review your long list and use it to create a shorter list of *five* underlined traits or qualities, one from each person you've chosen as a Hero.

Your list should now look something like this:

☞ Abraham Lincoln: Integrity

☞ My grandfather: Respect

☞ Spider-Man's Uncle Ben: Contribution

☞ Marie Curie: Self-Improvement

☞ Martin Luther King: Significance

Congratulations. You have just created a first-draft list of your core Values. That is a start. But it is not the end!

Question Five:
What Does the Second Draft of Your List Look Like?

Using your first-draft list, your next job is to check how well it matches up with the following four Value Categories and revise it so that it fulfills all four. You may need to go back and use words you have developed earlier in the process to do this.

☞ Which of the words on your list is your *foundational* Value? Foundational Values are the basis or framework on which everything else stands. They identify the one thing you will never, ever compromise on. (For Lincoln, that value was Integrity.) Foundational Values speak to your character.

☞ Which of the words on your list are *relational* Values? These Values affect the way in which two or more people behave toward and deal with each other. Notice that

Integrity can be expressed as both a foundational Value and a relational Value.

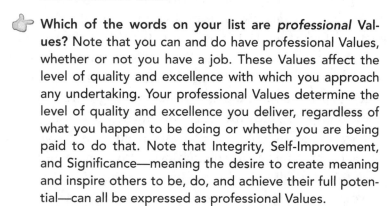 **Which of the words on your list are *professional* Values?** Note that you can and do have professional Values, whether or not you have a job. These Values affect the level of quality and excellence with which you approach any undertaking. Your professional Values determine the level of quality and excellence you deliver, regardless of what you happen to be doing or whether you are being paid to do that. Note that Integrity, Self-Improvement, and Significance—meaning the desire to create meaning and inspire others to be, do, and achieve their full potential—can all be expressed as professional Values.

Which of the words on your list are *community* Values? These Values affect how you feel about, participate in, and support your community. Note that Contribution can be expressed as a community Value and also as a relational Value governing your interactions with others—or both.

This part is important: **A great list of core Values ticks all four of these boxes.** Revise yours until it does. This may mean tweaking the number of core Values on your list. There is no right number of core Values, although I will say that if your list contains more than seven, it is likely to be unwieldy and hard to remember. Do your best to narrow the focus while retaining the meaning and significance.

Once your list does tick all four boxes, you have a viable second draft of your list of core Values. But that is not the end of the process!

Question Six:
What Is the Narrative for Each of Your Core Values?

Just writing down a list of words is not enough to establish your core Values—not by a long shot. For one thing, each word you have chosen needs to be clearly defined so that it is obvious what unique meaning it carries for *you*. What you mean by Integrity may be very different from what someone else means. Not only that—the meanings of your core Values are likely to become clearer to you over time. You need a Narrative. A Narrative, in this context, is a written statement of what you DO to make sure the Values show up in your world. The Narrative helps you get the key distinctions down on paper so that you can review them a month from now, a year from now, or a decade from now, and make whatever changes are necessary in light of your overall life experience and any new perspectives you've gained over time. In writing the Narrative and gaining clarity about what each Value means to you, you will also gain deeper insights on which Values fall into which of the four categories I have shared with you: foundational, relational, professional, and community. Remember, one Value can attach to one, several, or all four of the categories.

Here again, for illustration purposes, is the Narrative that supports my Values. Use it to get a clear sense of what a Narrative looks like. *Do not* use it as something you can cut and paste into a file and pretend it is your Narrative. *Do* use it as a model for bringing your own core Values to life.

My Values:

INTEGRITY

I make decisions based on the belief that my word is my bond and doing what is right is always the right thing to do. I commit to this no matter what.

RESPECT

I see all people as equal. I value other people's opinions, appreciate their beliefs, and recognize the importance of their priorities.

SIGNIFICANCE

I create meaning in my life and the lives of the people around me. I look for ways to create significance for my family. I make the effort to get to know people. I look for potential in the people with whom I come in contact. I encourage people. I participate in my community and work to make a difference.

Life is an adventure. I actively live that adventure when I live with integrity, respect, and significance.

"Be strong and resolute."

Remember: *Only when your actions align with your core Values are the Values yours.* If you look back at the end of a day and find you made *no* decisions that align with your core Values, there is something you need to fix. Values are not something that you want to achieve at some point in the future. They are right now.

Write your Core Value Narrative in your own words. See Chapter 14 for an example, but do not use my Narrative or anyone else's verbatim.

DO THIS BEFORE YOU MOVE ON

For each of your core Values, ask yourself: "How is this showing up in my life?"

For each of your core Values, ask yourself: "How is this NOT showing up in my life—and where could it be showing up more?"

Take two minutes each morning just to think about your Purpose, Mission, and Values, and how they match up with your decisions. Take one Value and think about how to incorporate it into everything you do that day.

Accountability Takeaways: Chapter 17

To identify your Values and create a powerful Values Narrative, ask yourself these questions:

- Who are my Heroes?

- Why are those people my Heroes?

- Where am I right now in relation to their qualities?

- What are their five most important traits?

- What does the next draft of my Values list look like?

- What is the Narrative for each of my core Values?

PART III

PUTTING ACCOUNTABILITY INTO ACTION

CHAPTER 18

WHAT NOW?

AT THIS POINT, if this book has done its job, you have a clear understanding of the following things:

👉 Accountability is all about commitments to people—relational commitments.

👉 Accountability is a way of thinking, not a way of doing. Specifically, it is how we think about people and how we think about our relationships with them.

👉 Accountability always starts with us. We must be accountable in order to inspire accountability in others.

👉 Accountability is not about controlling others. Accountability is also not about having to prove ourselves. Accountability is all about *interdependence*. We need other people to help us be our very best, and we need to help other people be their very best. In fact, in order to be our very best, we *must* help others be their very best.

👉 Accountability means working on being aligned with your own Purpose. Your Purpose is the *Why*, the reason you do the things you do. (By this point, you should have a clear, written Declaration of Purpose.)

👉 Accountability means working on being aligned with your own Mission. Your Mission is the *What*, your Purpose in action. (As you move forward into this final part of the book, you should also have a clear, written Mission Narrative.)

👉 Accountability means living your Values. Your Values are the *How*, the House Rules that guide your behavior even when no one is looking. (Before you continue with this part of the book, please be sure you have completed a clear, written Values Narrative.)

The question before us now is how to ensure that your Purpose, your Mission, and your Values exist as more than words on a page.

Our challenge—yours and mine—is to make sure these three things show up consistently in your interactions with others. We have to ensure that they are not just abstract concepts but that they actually lay the foundation for truly accountable relationships with all the people in your life. (Yes, I said *all*.) And the way we are going to do that is by means of the special relationship known as an Accountability Circle.

Someone who is in your Accountability Circle knows your Purpose, Mission, and Values as intimately as you do. By the same token, you know *their* Purpose, Mission, and Values as intimately as they do. If either of you notices the other person going off track, you each have a commitment to speak up, compassionately and constructively, about what you see. And the other person has a commitment to listen.

Notice that this critical relationship is rooted in *mutual commitment*.

The model for the Accountability Circle that I will be sharing with you is a shared set of agreements between two or more people connecting regularly to closely examine their commitments to each other and to the larger world. People who commit to take part in such discussions are Accountability Partners. The Accountability Partners in your life are special people. In this part of the book, we will be looking at the best ways for you to support those relationships.

Here is how the launch of your Accountability Circle could play out.

👉 **You finish this book, completing all the exercises and activities.** As a result, you have a clear sense of what your own Purpose, your own Mission, and your own Values look like in written form...and you are feeling empowered and more connected to your true self than you can ever remember feeling. You want that feeling to continue, and you want to share it with others, so...

👉 **You reach out to someone you trust, someone whom you believe would be a great Accountability Partner, and you give that person a copy of this book.** Do not ask them to buy it. Do not simply recommend it. This is a journey of positive change for both of you, and it is far too important to talk about it in hypothetical terms! Make your discussion with this person about something specific and tangible. Put a physical copy of this book into the person's hands—your own copy or a brand-new one—and then say something along the following lines: "Listen, this book had a huge impact on me. The idea of accountability is really powerful. It's all about keeping commitments to people and checking in regularly with an Accountability Partner about those commitments. I think it has the possibility to transform my life—and your life, too. *You need to read this.* I really want for us to do this together, and potentially I'd like to bring two or three other people into the discussion, people whom we both feel good about. If you want to do this, I want to do it with you. Can you read it, and can we talk about this next week?" If the person says, "Yes," you move on to the next phase of the discussion a week later.

👉 **A week later, you meet with your friend again.** You say, "Is this something you want to do?" IMPORTANT: The person cannot be part of your Accountability Circle if he or she has not read the book! If they do not understand what they are agreeing to, encourage them to *finish* reading the book...and move on to someone else while they do so! On the other hand, if the person *has* finished reading the book and is personally motivated to join your Circle, you are ready to proceed.

👉 **Check in on how much progress they have made in developing a written Declaration of Purpose, a Mission Narrative, and a Values Narrative.** You may need to say something like, "Before we can start, we both need to work through the exercises together and get that done." It is possible your friend may need some help in completing the exercises that appear in Chapters 10, 13, and 17. If so, give him or her that help. Once those exercises are finished and the results have been shared with you, your friend has officially become your Accountability Partner!

👉 **Once you are both clear on your Purpose, Mission, and Values, expand the Circle.** Say, "I have some ideas on one or two other people we may want to do this with." Make sure your Accountability Partner is comfortable with the idea of sharing his or her Purpose, Mission, and Values with these people. If so, get the new people to do all the same things you and your Accountability Partner have done...and schedule your first meeting. (I will share some thoughts on meeting logistics and topics in Chapter 19.)

👉 **If you can come up with only one person, do not let that stop you from taking part in an Accountability Circle.** Just know that there is an advantage if you choose to work with more than one person, for the simple reason that you will be able to have more than one voice weighing in on your weekly updates. This is an important consideration. Having more than one person who can let you know if you are going Off Purpose is extremely important. If all of your trusted Accountability Partners give you the same feedback, you will want to think long and hard before you dismiss that feedback. When two or more people you trust stop you in your tracks and tell you, "Hey, what you're planning on doing here doesn't sound like it lines up with your Purpose and your Values," that's powerful. I believe we each need that kind of "flashing red light" warning system. We need to know when more than one person in our Accountability Circle has flagged a problem. We run the red light at our own risk! There is a special power that comes with surrounding yourself with a special group of people who have your best interests in mind. If, however, you feel comfortable only with one Accountability Partner, you should have regular discussions with that person.

An important side note: I would not go above five people in an Accountability Circle. The discussions run the risk of becoming cumbersome at that point, and there is the possibility of people feeling as though their issues are not being addressed by the group.

PARTNER OR CANDIDATE?

As you put your Accountability Circle together, be careful not to confuse an Accountability Partner with an Accountability Candidate. An Accountability Partner is someone who has finished this book and has made an agreement with you to take part in regularly scheduled Accountability Circle meetings, the structure of which you will be learning about in Chapter 19. An Accountability Candidate is someone who has not yet finished reading this book and who has not yet completed all the activities connected with it but who wants to learn more about taking part in an Accountability Circle. They are two very different groups. *If the person with whom you are talking has not yet created a written Statement of Purpose, a Mission Narrative, and a Values Narrative, a meaningful discussion about accountability in your relationship, or in the larger world, is not yet possible.*

This is *not* a conversation between friends who are "just checking in" with one another, nor is it a business conversation in which your goal is to share tactical best practices with each other, even though both of those things may happen during conversations within the Accountability Circle. This is about who you are each showing up as in the world and whether you are each in full alignment with your Purpose, Mission, and Values.

There is an art to setting up and sustaining an ongoing relationship that produces such conversations. Mastering that art is partially a matter of following the guidance I will be sharing with you in this part of the book and partially a matter of trial and error. Choose carefully, and as you consider the various candidates, remember that your relationship with your Accountability Partners must be unlike any other relationships you have ever experienced. These relationships will be defined by vigorous, regular conversations about exactly how accountability is, or is not, manifesting in your life. This will not always be a comfortable conversation. But it will always be a safe and committed conversation, one you will come to find extremely valuable and important.

Your Accountability Partners are always going to be right in the middle of the most important events and decisions in your life, and they are always going to be committed to ensuring that you become the best possible version of yourself as you move forward. Your Accountability Partners are entitled to know what you are up to, and vice versa. You cannot help each other keep your commitments if you are not being truthful with each other about what you are doing! All of you will commit to speaking the truth, listening with compassion and patience, and responding with the truth. And all of you will grow as a result.

It should go without saying, then—but I will say it for the sake of absolute clarity—that your Accountability Partners must be chosen with great care. It is vitally important that you look closely at the character of the individual, not just at factors like how long you have known the person or the interests you may share. Some people have an inner circle that is based on chance or on factors like what kind of entertainment they enjoy. Accountable people choose their inner circle based on character and commitment.

This is your inner circle. Who gets to join it? That is one of the most important decisions you will ever make. Choose wisely. The Accountability Circle discussion is a special kind of conversation, one that requires the right people. It is worth taking the time to get the personnel right.

GET IT RIGHT!

 The Accountability Circle discussion is a special kind of conversation, one that requires the right people. Take the time to get the personnel right.

NOTHING IS OFF-LIMITS

In your discussions with your Accountability Partners, nothing—and I do mean nothing—should be considered off-limits. There is no pretending you have one set of Values for work, one set of Values for home, and a third set of Values for when you interact with people outside of those two environments. You have one set of Values, *period*. You are either living them or you are not. Not only that—you have one Purpose and one Mission. Your actions either support your Purpose and your Mission, or they do not.

Your Accountability Partners are here to help you figure out whether you are in alignment with what you have determined is truly important in your life. And vice versa. You are all here to ensure that there is no wiggle room.

SAY IT OUT LOUD

We come now to a very important point. It is quite common for people who are new to this process to feel hesitant about sharing personal material like their Purpose, Mission, and Values out loud in front of other people. It is easy to feel intimidated by the very act of sharing, even when we know that what is being shared is vitally important to our relationship with our Accountability Partners. Very often, the real reason we are hesitant to share our Purpose, Mission, and Values out loud is that we know, deep down inside, that once we share these things verbally with someone in our world, we must live by what we say. This is precisely the reason you *must* speak these words aloud. Speaking the words is what empowers you to live them in the moment!

All I can say to you, if you feel hesitation about talking openly to others about the important work you have done thus far, is that this hesitation to speak about **who you are, why you are here, and what you believe** represents both an obstacle that you can and must overcome… and an opportunity to turn your words into actions that transform your world. Your Accountability Partners are there to help you to overcome the obstacle and take full advantage of the opportunity.

MAKE KEY COMMITMENTS OUT LOUD

 The words we speak matter. Once we make a commitment out loud within the Accountability Circle, we are far more likely to honor it.

You must—repeat, *must*—use the Accountability Circle to practice sharing what you have learned and recorded in writing about your Purpose, Mission, and Values.

You must talk about these things with the people in your Circle and, in turn, hear them talk about their Purpose, their Mission, and their Values. This is simply non-negotiable.

Sharing this material within your Circle is a prelude—a warm-up, if you will—to the act of sharing it with the larger world. There is a reason you must be ready to get better and better at doing this kind of sharing: *speaking with others about who you are, what you are doing, and what you believe in is energizing.*

It may feel a little uncomfortable at first, but guess what? So was walking before you had figured out how to do that. So was driving a car. So was anything worth achieving.

If you keep your Purpose, Mission, and Values entirely to yourself, they are not working to their fullest potential for you or for anyone else in your life. But the moment you open up and share them with another person—one of your Accountability Partners, for instance— you will find that your focus will change, your level of commitment will intensify, and your ability to take action on what matters most in your world will be magnified in an exponential way.

Yes, it may feel intimidating for you to talk about this with other people right now, and you may have an excuse that seems to justify your not talking to them...but remember that if you are a member of an Accountability Circle, you are committed to moving beyond excuses.

So do that now. Commit to move beyond whatever excuse is keeping you from speaking directly to your Accountability Partners about the work you have already done. The minute you share what you have uncovered about yourself with others, your focus will change in that moment, and the Accountability Circle will become that much stronger.

ACCOUNTABILITY IS EVERY INTERACTION

When you share what is going on in your world, and your Accountability Partners share what is going on in their world, you are doing this to energize each other, to support each other, and to help each other be more fully accountable. You are doing this on the theory that accountability is every interaction and every minute of every day, starting with your interactions with your Accountability Partners and radiating outward.

So there is going to be a lot to talk about: personal issues, family issues, business issues, financial issues, and yes, even interactions with total strangers. You have to be ready to talk about how all of it connects to your Purpose, your Mission, and your Values. All of it is relevant. All of it connects. *All* of your choices impact your ability to follow through on your commitments.

You really can go off track in an instant, and stay off track, when you lose sight of your commitments in even a seemingly insignificant area. It is all significant! That is why this part of the book is here: to give you clarity about the most important commitments and to help you begin to establish the pattern of checking in regularly with your

Accountability Partners. That way, you can quickly get back on track about ANYTHING. It is very, very easy to make choices that do not align with our Purpose, Mission, and Values. One of the major reasons to take part in an Accountability Circle is to get better at noticing those choices when they occur.

Let me share an example that will illustrate exactly what I mean. A good friend of mine, Jon, has the stated Value of Peace. Recently, he told me on one of our Accountability Circle calls that since he and I had last spoken, he had had a situation where he had become frustrated and lost his temper with a customer service associate who was talking to him on the phone. Jon recognized that moment for what it was—a choice point where he had failed to live up to his own Value, and as a result of that choice, he had lost that Value. In that moment, Jon had not been living the Value of Peace. In order to feel that he was in alignment with his own Values, he had to acknowledge exactly what had happened and identify what he was going to do to avoid going off track again when he faced a similar situation.

Ultimately, we need to recognize that this is all a matter of mindfulness, a matter of being present in our own thought process. As Jon interacted with that customer service representative, he faced a choice point. In that instant, he made a choice. Unfortunately, the choice he made did not align with his stated Values. *That unaligned choice was a big deal, not something minor.* It was important for him to understand.

Jon realized that, and he brought it up within his Accountability Circle for discussion, and as a result, he got deeper clarity about the internal thought process that had led him to respond to that customer service person in a way that brought him out of alignment with his own Values. Once he understood and owned what had happened and took the steps appropriate for him to avoid repeating that kind of choice in the future, he told me, "I feel I am living my Value of Peace."

It is impossible to regain a Value you have lost if you are not mindful enough to recognize what caused you to lose it in the first place!

Noticing what choices we have made, why we made them, what the implications of those choices were, and what choices we can make now is a big part of what makes us human. You are not beating yourself up over a poor choice you made. You are simply noticing what happened and having a factual conversation within the Circle so you can all learn from each other's experiences. You are saying to yourself and to your Accountability Partners, "This is what happened, and this is how I am working on it." This is mindfulness in action. Over time, the goal is to notice the choice points as they are happening so that you can make aligned decisions the first time around, as opposed to stumbling around in the dark as though you had no Values at all!

An Accountability Circle works because it expresses mindfulness at the level of a small, mutually committed group. The essence of a good Accountability Circle discussion is two or more people saying to each other: "I trust you implicitly, and I trust your opinion. I need your help. I want you to help me be more accountable. Here is what I have been up to since we last talked. If you think I am off track, I really need to know about that." You start some back and forth around those issues. And you each accept that, when someone in the Circle says, "Hey, I think maybe you are out of alignment with the Values you've shared with me," it is time to listen. (Remember, too, that one of the core agreements of the Accountability Circle is that what its members share with each other is confidential and must remain within the Circle unless the person who shared it gives permission for it to be shared elsewhere.)

A BIG QUESTION

The kind of intimacy we are talking about here leads us to an obvious question: Should your spouse, romantic partner, or significant other be in your Accountability Circle? My short answer to that is: no. This person should certainly *know* your Purpose, your Mission, and your Values, and should be kept up to date about what you are working toward in your Accountability Circle. Why would you not want to share what you have learned about yourself with the one person who is closest to you and knows you best? This person can (and I would say *should*) be your Accountability Partner in life, but not in a group, since your relationship with your spouse is fundamentally different, and more intimate on every level, than the relationship you have with the Accountability Partners in your Circle. Your relationship with your spouse is unique. Because of that, your Accountability Partner relationship with your spouse should be one on one.

THE BIG IDEA...AND THE RELATIONAL COMMITMENTS THAT SUPPORT IT

You have reached a point in this book, I hope, where you can grasp the big idea behind the Accountability Circle:

An Accountability Circle is a safe place where you...

☞ get help from people you trust to remain committed to living your Values, Purpose, and Mission;

☞ help the members of your Circle live their Values, Purpose, and Mission;

and in so doing, each fulfill your potential as human beings by building a more accountable life and a more accountable world.

Make no mistake: This is an intense, focused, and purposeful discussion. This kind of discussion happens by means of ten specific relational commitments that all truly accountable people take on. Regardless of whether they call these commitments by the same names that I do, regardless of whether they even think of them as commitments, *this is what truly accountable people do.* They make these relational commitments in ten critical areas. They may not speak of them at all (except to Accountability Partners), but they keep those commitments.

KEEP YOUR COMMITMENTS

Accountability is about keeping our commitments to people. That starts in the Accountability Circle. There are ten specific relational commitments that all truly accountable people take on. Remember: We are responsible for things, but we are accountable to people!

Take a close look at each of these Accountability Commitments… notice that they are all relational, rather than tactical…and notice that they are *interrelated.* You cannot skip or minimize any of them and expect to live an accountable life. You have to implement the entire list.

COMMITMENT #1: COMMIT TO DISCOVER AND REALIZE YOUR POTENTIAL...AND TO HELP OTHERS REACH THEIRS

It is only when you are committed to being the best person you can possibly be that you can lead others to their potential and expect the best from them. This commitment begins with *you* and your potential...but it must extend to helping your Accountability Partners reach their full potential, too.

COMMITMENT #2: COMMIT TO THE TRUTH

Making a commitment to the truth means starting the search for dishonesty by looking in the mirror. It means acknowledging that we may lie to ourselves. When you notice one of your Accountability Partners not being truthful or hiding behind an excuse, you commit to speak up. When an Accountability Partner tells you that you are not being truthful, you commit to listen. When an Accountability Partner tells you that you are making an excuse that is keeping you from fulfilling your true potential, you commit to identify and move past the excuse.

COMMITMENT #3: COMMIT TO THE VALUES

Before you can ask one of your Accountability Partners, "Where is this Value showing up in your world?" YOU must first be clear on where YOUR Values are showing up in YOUR OWN LIFE. Are you? Do you, for instance, know what your Values are without checking to see what you wrote down? Are you comfortable talking about them?

COMMITMENT #4: COMMIT TO "IT'S ALL OF US"

When you commit to "It's all of us," you accept that you do not succeed unless the other person succeeds—and that if the other person fails, you fail. Start by making this commitment *explicitly* to your

Accountability Partners. They should make the same commitment to you. This commitment starts with your Accountability Partners, but it also ripples outward toward the larger world.

COMMITMENT #5: COMMIT TO EMBRACE FAULTS AND FAILURES AS WELL AS OPPORTUNITIES AND SUCCESSES

This commitment applies to your relationships with others and also to your relationship with yourself. In an Accountability Circle, you embrace both the best and the worst moments. Specifically, you speak up about your own shortcomings and see discussing them as opportunities for growth. Identifying your shortcomings does not mean you have to beat yourself up or be harsh with yourself in dealing with past mistakes. Being transparent about your errors and shortcomings in your interactions with other people builds trust. Lack of transparency about your errors and shortcomings always destroys trust. It takes time, practice, and commitment to develop the habit of being open with others about mistakes. The best and safest place to begin is with your Accountability Partners. Because we are not perfect, we do not expect our Accountability Partners, or any of the other people in our world, to be perfect. We understand that to be human is to be a work in process.

COMMITMENT #6: COMMIT TO SOUND FINANCIAL PRINCIPLES

This commitment is all about stewardship. That means setting up a sound financial plan, saving, and making contributions in areas that matter to you. Financially accountable people ask themselves constantly: *Does this investment really make sense for me?* Answering that question requires a serious, ongoing conversation. Be ready to have that conversation with your Accountability Partners.

COMMITMENT #7: COMMIT TO A SAFE SPACE

What you allow in your space, you condone. Are you ready to take on the commitment to create and sustain a safe physical, emotional, and psychological space for yourself and others? That means accepting that your interactions with others must be collaborative. That means they must not be driven by a desire to score points, exert dominance for the sake of exerting dominance, or get your ego stroked. Full disclosure: This takes practice. Start by making sure the space in which you and your Accountability Partners have your conversations is a safe space.

COMMITMENT #8: COMMIT TO "MY WORD IS MY BOND"

This commitment is a two-sided coin. One side of the coin is all about making decisions based on the principle that what you say must align with what you actually do. For instance, if you say that one of your Values is Honesty, then your company's business model cannot be built on deception. If you tell someone you are going to be there for them when they need you, then you need to be there for them when they need you. The other side of the coin is all about remembering that doing what you know in your heart to be right is *always* the right thing to do. The commitment to live a life in which your word is your bond is the commitment to live a life of Integrity. It is a commitment, not just to deliver on the explicit promises you make, but to strive to act in such a way that you would be ready, willing, and able to acknowledge your actions and your decisions in public if you were ever called upon to do so.

COMMITMENT #9: COMMIT TO STAND STRONG WHEN ALL HELL BREAKS LOOSE

Even when all hell breaks loose, you can be the stronghold in your own life, not the victim of people and circumstances. Within the Accountability Circle, this commitment means you and your Accountability Partners stay in touch and support each other even when things get busy and even when there is a crisis. Making this commitment to an Accountability Partner means you are there for them when all hell breaks loose in their life, and they know they can count on you for support, no matter what. Notice that if you are not in touch with and supporting your Accountability Partners on a mutually agreed-upon, mutually convenient schedule, you are not fulfilling this commitment. If something else is always more important than consistent discussions within the Circle, you are not committed to standing strong for your Accountability Partners.

COMMITMENT #10: COMMIT TO A GOOD REPUTATION

Your reputation is defined by others based on your actions. When your actions show that you are fulfilling the commitments you have just been reading about, then you are seen as a person with a good reputation. Never make a decision that would harm that reputation! Note that committing to a good reputation does not mean boasting, bragging, or writing up a great press release. It means aligning consistently, in both word and deed, on the nine commitments you have just read, nothing more and nothing less. If you do that much, your reputation within your Accountability Circle—and everywhere else—will take care of itself. If you do not, your reputation will suffer. It is as simple as that.

What I have shared here is a very brief summary of each of these critical commitments. For a much deeper dive on the ten Accountability Commitments, see my book *I Am Accountable. (Visit https://samsilverstein.com/shop/.)*

Accountability Takeaways: Chapter 18

The Accountability Circle discussion is a special kind of conversation, one that requires the right people. Take the time to get the personnel right.

The words we speak matter. Once we make a commitment out loud within the Accountability Circle, we are far more likely to honor it.

Accountability is about keeping our commitments to people. That starts in the Accountability Circle. There are ten specific relational commitments that all truly accountable people take on. Remember: We are responsible for things, but we are accountable to people!

1. Commit to discover and realize your potential...and to help others reach theirs.

2. Commit to the truth.

3. Commit to the Values.

4. Commit to "It's all of us."

5. Commit to embrace faults and failures as well as opportunities and successes.

6. Commit to sound financial principles.

7. Commit to a safe space.

8. Commit to "My word is my bond."

9. Commit to stand strong when all hell breaks loose.

10. Commit to a good reputation.

CHAPTER 19

THREE BEST PRACTICES
THAT SUPPORT THE ACCOUNTABILITY CIRCLE

AT THIS POINT, you are probably saying to yourself, "Okay—where do we go from here? Once we have identified the people in our Accountability Circle and we have all completed the up-front work, what do we actually *do*?"

What I am about to share with you is a summary of what has worked for me and my Accountability Partners to create an environment that made it possible for each of us to achieve what we wanted to achieve. These three best practices are what allow an Accountability Circle to stay on track, operate effectively, and keep everyone focused on what matters most to the members.

Best Practice One: Have a Discussion about Basic Meeting Commitments.

You should probably begin with a discussion about how often you will be meeting. I strongly recommend starting with the goal of having a call or meeting at least once a week. I would schedule at least half an hour. In my experience, an hour-long session once a week is ideal for a group of three or four people, at least in the early going. Less frequent than that is simply not effective, and more frequent may give some members of the circle "meeting fatigue." I would also discuss the *hows* and *wheres* of the meeting: face to face and in person (early in the morning at a conveniently located coffee shop, for instance) is far preferable to doing a conference call or a video call. That being said, a conference call or video call held consistently is far better than an in-person meeting that happens irregularly. Find a pattern that feels comfortable to all of you, give it a try, and see how it goes. Other basic meeting commitments that are important to discuss include the commitment to give the discussion full attention while it is going on and the commitment to give the scheduled weekly meeting priority over other nonemergency events. This is not a trial period. You are all really doing this. So if you are doing it, do it. Commit to show up on time unless there is a genuine emergency. Commit to work together as a group when logistical questions arise (which they will). Commit to make it as easy as possible for everyone to take part. Let me suggest that establishing a strong mutual commitment to show up on time is particularly important for the success of the group. This time is special. If the Circle is not important enough for someone to schedule other things around it for an hour or so once a week, it may not be time for that person to be part of the Circle.

Best Practice Two: Identify the First Facilitator; Understand What the Facilitator Does and Does Not Do.

The person who facilitates the Accountability Circle does the following:

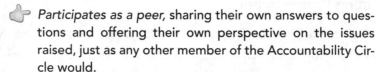 *Participates as a peer,* sharing their own answers to questions and offering their own perspective on the issues raised, just as any other member of the Accountability Circle would.

Makes sure everyone has the chance to speak. The facilitator gives people who have a pressing need a little extra time and the opportunity to share what they need to share with the group.

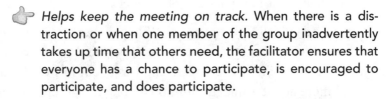 *Helps keep the meeting on track.* When there is a distraction or when one member of the group inadvertently takes up time that others need, the facilitator ensures that everyone has a chance to participate, is encouraged to participate, and does participate.

Reminds people, tactfully, that feedback based on experience is more valuable than feedback based on opinion. Here is an example of focusing on opinion: "I don't think that's a good idea." An example of focusing on the experience might sound like this: "I would be hesitant about doing such-and-such because I had a similar experience along the following lines that didn't turn out well. Can I tell you about it?"

Concludes the meeting on time. Respecting time agreements is an important part of the facilitator's job.

Makes sure people know when and where the next meeting is. This can be as simple as, "See you here next week at the same time" (if that's the agreement).

Helps the group identify the next facilitator. It shouldn't be the same person all the time.

Here is what the facilitator *does not* do:

Take personal control of the meeting. This is a conversation among peers. It is not the facilitator's job to announce whether anyone else's responses are acceptable or unacceptable. The basic guideline to follow here is *Speak your truth and listen without judgment as others speak theirs.*

Discourage people from participating. The facilitator must not keep people from talking who want to talk. The only exceptions to this are impartial redirections in the interest of time or relevance.

☞ *Make it all about them.* If the Circle "happens" to focus exclusively or mostly on the issues of the facilitator, that facilitator has not done the job correctly.

These broad guidelines are just a start. They are here to make it easy for you and others to lead the meeting. As time goes by, you will find that your Accountability Circle is less and less about formal dos and don'ts and more about a shared intuition among the group members about what usually happens to make the session work.

Best Practice Three: Download and Follow the Accountability Circle Discussion Guide.

Work with the following simple list of "big picture" discussion items for your weekly Accountability Circle meetings. You can download a printable copy of the Discussion Guide at https://samsilverstein.com/acguide.

THE ACCOUNTABILITY CIRCLE DISCUSSION GUIDE

FOR THE FACILITATOR: Start the meeting with a quick update. Everyone gets to say briefly what is going on in their life and also gets the opportunity for an "ask": something they need input on or assistance with from the group. You can then move on to that week's general discussion topic and its accompanying questions, as outlined below. Each member should make an effort to address each question.

This Discussion Guide gives you thirteen weeks' worth of topics. If you choose, you can repeat the cycle, which would mean that each of the topics would be addressed four times over the course of a given year.

WEEK ONE:
WHAT IS MY PURPOSE? WHAT IS YOURS?

Note: This first meeting may well need to go longer than sixty minutes. I recommend allotting at least ninety minutes.

Your Purpose is the reason you are here, phrased in the form of service that you render to others. Your Purpose is your Why.

By this point, you will have each done a fair amount of work on your Statement of Purpose. Even so, you should each be ready to refine what you have written and receive feedback from the Circle about it. Members of the Circle should feel free to ask questions and propose constructive suggestions about each person's written Statement of Purpose. If you find that yours needs refining and revision, you can get help with that during this meeting. If you and the members of your Circle feel that your Purpose is hitting the mark, you can use this session to help others to find their own clarity.

The words of your Purpose cannot be considered as "set in stone." The way you express your Purpose may change over time, as your life changes.

Questions to cover during this first, vitally important Accountability Circle session include:

👉 What is your Purpose? (Share what you have written with the group.)

👉 Whom does your Purpose serve?

👉 Why did you select this as your Purpose?

👉 Why did you choose to articulate it in this specific way?

👉 Where has/does your Purpose show up in your life?

👉 Where do you want it to show up more fully?

👉 If you live this Purpose consistently, what does that look like, how does your life change, and how does it feel?

WEEK TWO:
WHAT IS MY MISSION? WHAT IS YOURS?

Your Mission is your Purpose in ACTION.

During this session, members of the Circle should feel free to ask questions and propose constructive suggestions about each person's written Mission Narrative. Bear in mind too that if your Mission never attracts or inspires anyone, you need to look closely at whether you have identified the right Mission!

Questions to cover during this Accountability Circle session include:

👉 What is your Mission? (Share your Mission Narrative with the group.)

👉 How does your Mission align with your Purpose?

👉 What are you most excited about in your Mission?

👉 Whom does your Mission serve?

👉 What are you doing to put this Mission into action?

👉 What kinds of Allies do you hope to attract to join your Mission?

👉 What steps are you taking to make that happen?

WEEK THREE:
WHAT ARE MY VALUES? WHAT ARE YOURS?

Your core Values state your principles and your standards of behavior—what is important in your life. They are the HOW.

There will inevitably come a time when we make a decision that goes against our Values. The key question in this situation is: Did we make the decision knowing full well that we were going against the Values? If the answer is yes, we have a problem, because that answer suggests we do not actually value what we said we value. If we simply lose sight of the Value in the heat of the moment and feel regret at having done so, the members of our Accountability Circle can help us to see that, own what happened, and quickly fix it by doing whatever is necessary to correct the mistake and take the steps to keep it from happening again. We share these moments not just for our own benefit but for the benefit of the others in the Circle. Our attitude is: "I am not always perfect in honoring my own Values; I will be here for you when you are not perfect in upholding yours."

Questions to cover during this Accountability Circle session include:

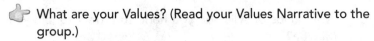 What are your Values? (Read your Values Narrative to the group.)

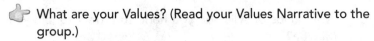 Why did you choose these Values?

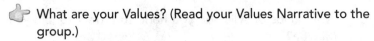 Where are they showing up in your life?

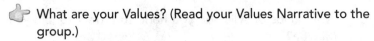 Where are they not showing up that you would like to see them show up?)

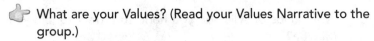 Under what circumstances have you made choices in the past that have compromised your Values?

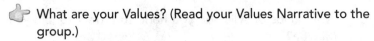 Are you committed to living these Values at the level of "non-negotiable"?

Does the organization for which you work align with these Values? How do you know one way or the other?

 What would you do if you were called on to do something at work that violated your Values?

WEEK FOUR:
COMMITMENT TO DISCOVER AND REALIZE MY POTENTIAL...AND TO HELP OTHERS REACH THEIRS

This commitment reminds us that we cannot be our very best unless we are helping others be their very best. Fulfilling this commitment is a trait of all great leaders, whether they have a formal leadership spot in some team or organization or they are simply leading by example in their own lives, without a specific job title. Notice that the list of Accountability Commitments begins with one that directly emphasizes the idea of *service*.

Questions to cover during this Accountability Circle session include:

 How is this commitment showing up in your life?

 How is it showing up in your relationships with family members?

 How is it showing up in your professional relationships?

 How is it showing up in your relationships with the people in this room?

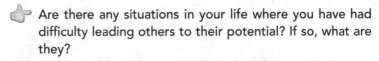 Are there any situations in your life where you have had difficulty leading others to their potential? If so, what are they?

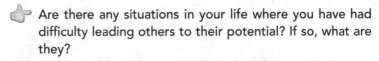 What do you need to do more of if you are going to be more effective in discovering and leading others to their potential?

WEEK FIVE:
COMMITMENT TO THE TRUTH

Lying and accountability cannot coexist. When we take on this commitment, we accept that seeking and speaking truth may not always be easy, but an accountable relationship is impossible without it.

Questions to cover during this Accountability Circle session include:

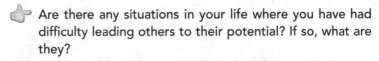 How is this commitment showing up in your life?

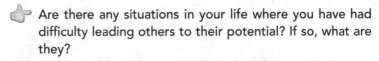 Do you honor this commitment even when it seems more convenient not to do so? When have you done that?

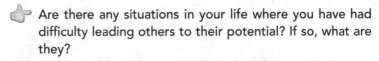 Is there a time when you find it challenging to honor this commitment? If so, how do you address that?

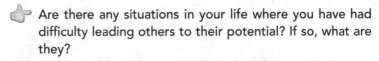 How do you respond when others in your presence are not committed to truth?

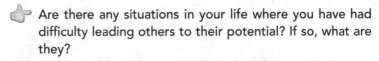 What is an example of a time when you spoke an important, difficult truth in a way that was easy for someone to hear?

WEEK SIX:
COMMITMENT TO THE VALUES

Your core Values state your principles and your standards of behavior—what is important in your life. They are the HOW.

Week Three was about formulating your Values. This week is about *living* your Values. Note that if there is no action or decision in support of a Value, you cannot say that you are living it. If the Values you identified in Week Three have led to no actions or decisions in support of those Values over the past weeks, it may be time to get help from the Circle in revising your list of Values or changing how you make decisions. Do not resist this; it is a sign of growth and discovery.

Questions to cover during this Accountability Circle session include:

- 👉 Where have your Values been showing up in your life? How do you know?

- 👉 What have these Values been producing in your life? How do you know?

- 👉 Where are you struggling with one or more of your Values? And if you are struggling, why are you struggling?

- 👉 How are your Values showing up in your relationships with others?

- 👉 Have you ever had a Values clash with someone? If so, how did you handle it?

- 👉 Have you discussed your Values directly with your spouse or significant other? If not, why not? If so, what was their response?

WEEK SEVEN:
COMMITMENT TO "IT'S ALL OF US"

When you commit to "It's all of us," you accept that you do not succeed unless the other person succeeds—and you accept that if the other person fails, you fail. This commitment starts with the people in your Accountability Circle. It extends outward until it eventually encompasses the entire human family. It may take some time for you to get to the point where you take on the commitment at that level, but that does not change the nature of the commitment.

Questions to cover during this Accountability Circle session include:

👉 How do others around you feel when you are fully living this commitment?

👉 Where is this commitment showing up in your life? How do you know?

👉 Where could you be living it more fully?

👉 Are you willing to live this commitment on behalf of everyone with whom you come in contact? If not, why not?

👉 Describe how you feel when someone around you is living this commitment in regard to you.

👉 Describe how you feel when someone is NOT living this commitment in regard to you.

WEEK EIGHT:
COMMITMENT TO EMBRACE FAULTS AND FAILURES AS WELL AS OPPORTUNITIES AND SUCCESSES

Living this commitment means you embrace both your best and worst moments. You speak up about your own shortcomings, and you see discussing them as opportunities for growth. You do not judge others based on their worst moments.

Failure is a part of human life. We all learn from failure. Accepting this fact supports our commitment to support each other's growth and development.

Taking on this commitment means taking on the mindset of "I am not perfect, and I do not expect you to be perfect."

Questions to cover during this Accountability Circle session include:

☞ Where is this commitment showing up in your life? How do you know?

☞ Where could you be living it more fully?

☞ Describe the most recent time when someone failed to attain an objective you felt could have and should have been attained. How did you respond?

☞ How do you deal with faults and weaknesses of those with whom you come in contact? Do you ever judge the people around you based on their mistakes or shortcomings?

☞ When was the last time you shared one of your mistakes or weaknesses with someone else? If you cannot think of such a time, why is that?

How does your transparency about your own mistakes and/or shortcomings impact your relationships with other people?

WEEK NINE:
COMMITMENT TO SOUND FINANCIAL PRINCIPLES

This commitment is all about stewardship and making wise decisions with our financial resources. We come to this world empty-handed. We leave it empty-handed. In between, it is our job to maintain "our" resources responsibly—including, but not limited to, financial resources.

We all have different means. That is fine. The big question here is, how do we go about making responsible financial decisions based on the realities of our own situation? How do we protect ourselves and the people who are counting on us to honor this commitment? It is possible that we may need to bring in professionals to help us with those choices. The Circle can help us determine whether or not this is the case, and if so, what steps we should take.

Questions to cover during this Accountability Circle session include:

 Where is this commitment showing up in your life? How do you know?

 Where could you be living it more fully?

 Do you live below your means? What, if any, are the challenges you face in doing so?

👉 Would the advice and guidance of a professional be able to help you to do a better job of taking on this commitment? If so, how?

👉 Do you have a financial plan? If not, what is keeping you from having one?

👉 How is giving showing up as a part of your financial plan?

WEEK TEN:
COMMITMENT TO A SAFE SPACE

This commitment is about creating and sustaining an environment of physical, emotional, and psychological safety. What we allow in our space, we condone. When we take on this commitment, we embrace the importance of personal safety, collaboration, and dialogue in *all* our interactions and *all* our circles, not just the Accountability Circle. But we start by making sure the Accountability Circle itself is a safe space. Bias, discrimination, and the habit of passing judgment keep us from creating a safe place for everyone.

Questions to cover during this Accountability Circle session include:

👉 Where is this commitment showing up in your life? How do you know?

👉 Where could you be living it more fully?

👉 When was the last time you were in a space that did not feel safe? What happened?

👉 Were you ever in a place where someone you were with was made to feel "less than"—and you knew it? How did you react then? How would you react the next time that happens?

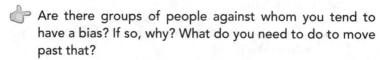 Are there groups of people against whom you tend to have a bias? If so, why? What do you need to do to move past that?

Do you ever tell stories or jokes that poke fun at someone for who they are or what they believe?

Where does diversity show up in your life—not just in terms of other people's external appearances, but in terms of thoughts and beliefs and outlooks? Where could it show up more?

WEEK ELEVEN:
COMMITMENT TO "MY WORD IS MY BOND"

This commitment reminds us that what we say must align with what we do. It also reminds us that there is a difference between *tactical* failures (situations where we have taken on a task and we experience a breakdown in fulfilling it) and *commitment* failures (situations where we make a conscious choice to step aside from a relational commitment). The former is to be expected from time to time, and it is usually something we can fix on our own with quick, thoughtful action and good communication. The latter, however, is a sign of a bigger problem, one that needs to be addressed within the Accountability Circle. Relational commitments are no matter what.

Questions to cover during this Accountability Circle session include:

Where is this commitment showing up in your life? How do you know?

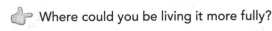 Where could you be living it more fully?

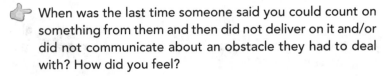 When was the last time someone said you could count on something from them and then did not deliver on it and/or did not communicate about an obstacle they had to deal with? How did you feel?

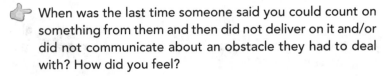 When is it difficult to deliver on your word? When you find a way to deliver on your word in those tough times, how do you think the people for whom you deliver feel?

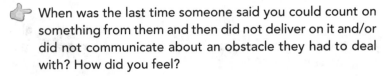 What happens when you make a promise and then find out there is an obstacle to keeping that promise that no one could have foreseen? What do you do?

WEEK TWELVE:
COMMITMENT TO STAND STRONG WHEN ALL HELL BREAKS LOOSE

This commitment is all about being there when people need you. There will be tough times in life. When we take on this commitment, we take on the decision to give people the support they need when they need it most, even if that is not convenient or easy.

Questions to cover during this Accountability Circle session include:

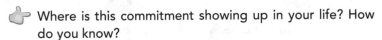 Where is this commitment showing up in your life? How do you know?

 Where could you be living it more fully?

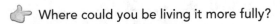 What was a time when you were going through an unexpected crisis and someone did something that was not

convenient or easy in order to support you? How did that make you feel?

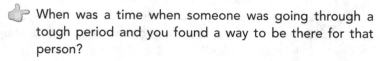 When was a time when someone was going through a tough period and you found a way to be there for that person?

Who counts on you during tough times?

On whom do you count during tough times?

WEEK THIRTEEN:
COMMITMENT TO A GOOD REPUTATION

This commitment reminds us that our actions matter—not just in the outcomes we deliver today, but in what people say about us, our organization, and our team tomorrow. If we are serious about taking on and honoring the other critical relational commitments we have discussed in the Circle, then our reputation will take care of itself. If we are not serious about those commitments, word about that will inevitably get around.

Questions to cover during this Accountability Circle session include:

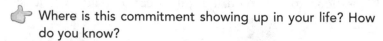 Where is this commitment showing up in your life? How do you know?

Where could you be living it more fully?

Describe a recent decision where the choice you made could have impacted your reputation. When are you likely to be faced with such a decision again?

👉 When has your reputation affected someone else's reputation?

👉 When have you acted in a way that helped maintain someone else's good reputation? Why did you decide to do that?

👉 Have you ever made a personal decision that may have tarnished your own or someone else's reputation?

👉 What can you do *daily* to help protect your reputation?

Accountability Takeaways: Chapter 19

There are three critical best practices that support the Accountability Circle. They are:

- **Best Practice One:** Have a discussion about basic meeting commitments.

- **Best Practice Two:** Identify the first facilitator; understand what the facilitator does and does not do.

- **Best Practice Three:** Download and follow the Accountability Circle Discussion Guide (available at https://samsilverstein.com/acguide).

CHAPTER 20

THE ART OF EXCEEDING YOUR OWN EXPECTATIONS

NOT LONG AGO, Karen, the wife of my Accountability Partner, Mike, said to me in a lighthearted tone, "I think you talk to my husband more than I do. But you know what? The truth is, your presence in his life—in our life—is very dear and precious to us. Mike is a better person because of his relationship with you."

I got a little choked up. I was deeply honored and humbled when I heard those words. I realized that what she had just told me was a part—but only a part—of the proof that our Accountability Circle was (and remains) a success. When the loved ones of your Accountability Partners celebrate the process into which you have been investing your time, effort, and energy, you certainly have reason to celebrate.

But that is not the whole story. There is another very important takeaway here that I want to be sure to highlight. So far, I have shared only half of the equation.

The truth is, *I am a better person because of Mike's relationship with me.* He has helped me achieve things of which I did not even realize I was capable. I am a better person because of all my Accountability Partners. That is the beautiful thing about an Accountability Circle: it benefits everyone it touches. It makes each engaged participant a better person. If it did not do that, it would be an indication that there was a problem within the Circle. And when it does do that, it is a blessing.

As you move forward and begin to implement the concepts and strategies I have shared with you in this book, my challenge to you is a simple one: never forget that in order to achieve our own potential, we must help other people be their very best...and we must accept their help in becoming our very best.

With that powerful principle in mind, let me share a few closing thoughts with you.

I realize that if you wanted to, you could take what you have read here, focus only on the parts that seemed most important or relevant to your world, and then try to implement those changes all on your own, without creating any Accountability Partnerships. You could follow the steps I have laid out to discover your Purpose, identify your Mission, and determine and establish your Values. And you know what? You would probably see some improvements. If you just lived what you have learned in these pages all by yourself, you could probably make significant strides and see some important changes taking root in your life. But if you made the effort to build your own Accountability Circle, you would have the potential to do *much more than that*. You would experience what I have experienced—namely, the ability to radically exceed your understanding of your own potential.

You would achieve things that you once thought you were incapable of doing. And that is what I want for you.

You are capable of so much more than what you believe you are capable of right now. If you want your life to exceed your own expectations, if you want it to be truly great, then *involve other people*. Share this book with them. Share this way of life with them. And always bear in mind that the responsibility for sustaining the depth and value of the relationship lies on us. If we are willing to be transparent, open up, and share the truths of our life, we can make truly amazing things happen. And we can leave what we once believed were the borders that defined our capacity to achieve and contribute far, far behind.

In the end, this book is not so much about accountability as it is about being a part of a global Accountability Movement. This is about you and me changing our lives, our communities, and our world because we choose to be accountable and to help others be accountable also. The Accountability Movement is all about us as individuals first being accountable in our life and then stepping up to build accountable organizations and communities. Ultimately, our outcome is to build a more accountable world—a place where we as people see our fellow human beings differently, we commit to them differently, and we achieve a different result. I hope you will take part in that Movement…and I hope you will stay in touch by subscribing to my newsletter, The Accountability Zone. You can subscribe for free at https://samsilverstein.com/connect/.

Join us!

Accountability Takeaways: Chapter 20

Join the Accountability Movement. Spread the word about accountability in your community.

ABOUT **THE AUTHOR**

SAM SILVERSTEIN is founder and CEO of Sam Silverstein, Incorporated, an accountability think tank dedicated to helping companies create an organizational culture that prioritizes and inspires accountable leaders. By helping organizations develop what they believe in, clarify their mission, and understand what is in their control, Sam works to make this a more accountable world. He is the author of several books, including *No More Excuses, Non-Negotiable, No Matter What, The Success Model, Making Accountable Decisions, The Lost Commandments,* and *I Am Accountable.* He speaks internationally, having worked with teams of companies, government agencies, communities, and organizations both big and small, including Kraft Foods, Pfizer, the United States Air Force, and United Way. Sam is the past president of the National Speakers Association.

Book Sam Silverstein
To Speak At Your Next Event

Contact Us

Sam Silverstein, Incorporated
121 Bellington Lane
St. Louis, Missouri 63141
info@SamSilverstein.com
(314) 878-9252

To Order More Copies of
The Accountability Circle:

www.samsilverstein.com

Follow Sam

www.twitter.com/samsilverstein

www.youtube.com/samsilverstein

www.linkedin.com/in/samsilverstein

www.instagram.com/samsilverstein

www.facebook.com/silversteinsam

No More Excuses | Making Accountable Decisions | The Success Model | I Am Accountable

Other books by **SAM SILVERSTEIN** available <u>everywhere books are sold.</u> or www.SamSilverstein.com

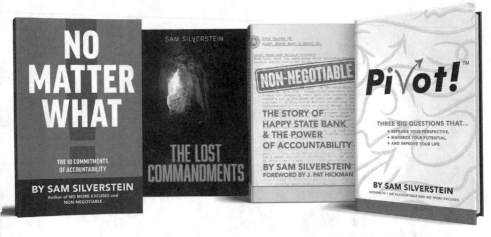

No Matter What | The Lost Commandments | Non Negotiable | Pivot!